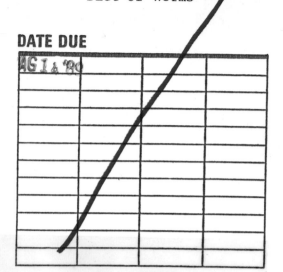
hARPER ✸ ᴛoRChBOOKS

A reference-list of Harper Torchbooks, classified
by subjects, is printed at the end of this volume.

LUTHER'S PROGRESS
to the
DIET OF WORMS

by
GORDON RUPP

HARPER TORCHBOOKS
THE CLOISTER LIBRARY
HARPER & ROW, PUBLISHERS
NEW YORK AND EVANSTON

TO
MY WIFE

LUTHER'S PROGRESS TO THE DIET OF WORMS

Introduction to the Torchbook edition
copyright © 1964 by Gordon Rupp

Printed in the United States of America.

This book was originally published in 1951 by S.C.M. Press Limited,
London, and is here reprinted by arrangement.

First HARPER TORCHBOOK edition published 1964 by Harper & Row, Publishers,
Incorporated, 49 East 33rd Street, New York, N.Y. 10016

CONTENTS

Introduction to the Torchbook edition　　　　1

Introduction　　　　7

I　YOUNG LUTHER　　　　9

II　MR. FEARING　　　　26

III　*'IN EXITU ISRAEL'*　　　　36

IV　THE HUBBUB　　　　48

V　GREAT ARGUMENT　　　　59

VI　THE REFORMER　　　　71

VII　THE KNIGHT OF FAITH　　　　92

Epilogue　　　　103

Index　　　　109

INTRODUCTION TO THE
TORCHBOOK EDITION

Luther's Progress to the Diet of Worms was written soon after World War II when there had inevitably been a slowing down of Luther studies, particularly in Germany. The last decade has seen a great stepping up of their pace. Two great international congresses have been held, at Aarhus in Denmark and at Münster in Germany, to consider some of the latest problems of this intricate field of scholarship. The *Luther Yearbook* (edited by Professor Franz Lau of Leipzig) continues to list year by year the number of publications dealing directly or indirectly with the life, thought, and influence of Martin Luther; these now top the figure of 600 annually, and though many of them are slight articles many others are printed volumes and substantial monographs. It has to be confessed that of the printing of theses there is no end: as the learned studies pour out of universities in Germany, Scandinavia, and America there is inevitably a tedious amount of repetition, so that the reader needs a guide to what *not* to read, and often would be far more profitably engaged in reading Luther for himself.

And it is in this respect, the availability of Luther for English readers who lack what may be called the "sacred" languages of German and Latin, that these last years have brought a revolution. The change has been made by the launching of the great American edition of the *Works of Martin Luther*, in 55 volumes, under the editorship of Dr. Lehmann and Professor Pelikan. Though in such a great enterprise there are bound to be variations in the quality of the editing and translating, the project is already an achievement which British scholars must hail with admiration and respect. The influence of great teachers like Roland Bainton, Wilhelm

1

Pauck, Theodore Tappert, and others is bearing fruit in a generation of American Luther scholars who combine theological perspective with the technical linguistic equipment. The great new edition puts a mass of lively, first-hand documents at the disposal of historians, theologians, and students. The four volumes devoted to the *Career of the Reformer* themselves constitute a major event in the Englishizing of Luther. We now have before us major theological documents, Luther's extended exposition of his 95 Theses, and the account of his important dealings with Cardinal Cajetan: the pregnant and profound *Against Latomus,* so important for the evaluation of Luther's doctrine of the relation between justification and the work of grace in the soul: the devastating polemic of *Against the Heavenly Prophets,* a formidable disposal of the errors of the left wing radicals, and incidentally of their modern admirers. Of the volumes so far published the most impressive is volume 37, devoted to Luther's eucharistic treatises of 1527-8, admirably edited by Dr. Robert H. Fischer. There are also important volumes devoted to his doctrines of Word and Sacraments, Church and ministry, and a wide selection from his sermons and expository lectures.

But the American edition of Luther's works does not exhaust the new material. Three recent volumes in the transatlantic venture, the "Library of Christian Classics," are devoted to Luther's writings. The first, *Letters of Spiritual Counsel* (edited by Theodore Tappert), is an admirable miscellany, perhaps the best book to lend anybody who wants to get the flavour of Luther's character and mind. Two further volumes contain Luther's lectures as a young Professor, with his *Commentary on Romans* (selections edited by Wilhelm Pauck) and with his other early lectures (edited by Canon J. Atkinson). In England, James Clarke has published new editions of older translations, the famous *Commentary on Galatians*—so influential in English history, not least on John Bunyan and Charles Wesley—(edited by P. S. Watson) and *The Bondage of the Will* (edited by James Packer). Recently a selection from Luther's *Meditations on the Gospels* has been translated by Roland Bainton; it is an excellent introduction to Luther and the reader will find much to delight and move him in these comments, which are often profound and always luminous with poetry and humour. Of late, English translations of the admirable monographs on Luther by Gerhard Ritter and Franz Lau also have appeared.

Luther's subtle teaching about spiritual and civil government, *The Two Kingdoms*, has been the subject of intermittent debate for centuries. In 1953, a learned and provocative study, *Lex Charitatis*, by Johannes Haeckel, sparked off a lively debate about the place of law in Luther's teaching on this subject. Important questions about Luther's teaching in relation to scholastic theology must wait until fifteenth century studies are more advanced. Among the more useful discussions in English is B. A. Gerrish's *Grace and Reason;* in German there is a more perceptive essay on the same theme, *Ratio und Fides*, by B. Lohse. The Danish scholar Leif Crane has contributed a massive examination of Luther's theses against the Schoolmen (published in 1517), with special reference to the famous Tübingen theologian, Gabriel Biel, who was the teacher of Luther's teachers. Most recently published is a work by H. A. Oberman, of the Harvard Divinity School, *The Harvest of Medieval Theology*, a study of Biel which is to be followed by further volumes about the relation of Biel's teaching to Luther and to the Reformation.

But the major event of the last few years has been another round in the ever-continuing debate about Luther's "breakthrough" in the meaning of the Righteousness of God (*Justitia Dei*). The great achievement of the "Luther Renaissance" in the first part of the twentieth century was the discovery, editing, and publishing of the mass of material from which Luther lectured at Wittenberg (1509-17). Naturally enough, research centered on the intriguing questions raised by the interpretation of this new evidence, and on the Young Luther. There was a parallel between the search for the historical Luther and the Biblical quest of the historical Jesus, for research in both cases pursued the historical method, relating events to the documents viewed in a strict philological context. It was inevitable that scholars should turn in this direction for the answer to the old problems raised by Luther's famous autobiographical fragment published in 1545, towards the end of his life. Therein he declared that he had been held up from exploring the world of Pauline thought by the concept (in *Romans* 1) of the "Righteousness of God" (*Justitia Dei*), which he had been taught to interpret as the punishing justice of God. The breakthrough came for him when he realized that Paul is speaking of another kind of righteousness, one which is God's merciful gift in which he saves and forgives us in Christ. Two essays by Erich Vogelsang were landmarks in the new discussion. Vogelsang suggested that Luther's realization occurred when he came to apply to the exegesis of the *Psalms* two of the four mediaeval exegetical schemes, the so-called "Literal-prophetic" interpretation in terms of Christ and the tropological which referred to the inward work of God in the individual soul. A combination of these two references to the *Justitia Dei*, he suggested, resulted in Luther's new conception: a righteousness displayed in Christ and given to the soul in faith. He thought to find evidence of the new conception in *Psalm* 70-1 in Luther's lectures, and dated the discovery 1513-4. And although his thesis was shaken by later investigations, notably that by Wenndorf, a good many scholars agreed that the discovery must be dated in this period, and certainly before the outbreak of the church struggle in 1517.

Lately, there has been a reversal of this trend (and perhaps here there is a parallel with the Bultmann era in Biblical studies). A series of essays by W. Link, U. Saarnivara, A. Peters, and others has appeared which would seek a later date (returning to the ancient interpretation of the 1545 *Fragment* which superficially suggests 1518-9 as the date of the discovery). The most impressive of these essays is that of Ernst Bizer's *Fides ex auditu*. His criticism of Vogelsang is indeed damaging; he argues learnedly and powerfully that what we have in Luther's lectures on *Psalms, Romans, Galatians,* and *Hebrews* (1513-7) is still really within a Catholic framework. Luther's real change of mind he finds evidenced in the critical months of the widening church battle, especially in Luther's battles with Cardinal Cajetan and with John Eck in which for the first time he related the doctrine of justification to the Word and the promises of God to the hearing of faith. Bizer's work is a permanent contribution to Luther studies, for he makes clear that Luther's thought is in movement, in development, during all these years, and he offers important evidence as to the character of Luther's theological discoveries during the exciting period of 1518-9. But brilliant as the attempted demonstration is, it merits the 1961 riposte which came from Regin Prenter, one of the great Scandinavian interpreters of Luther in our time. Prenter's book, *The Merciful Judge* (*Der Barkherzige Richter*), not only did not accept Bizer's late date but also damagingly assaulted Vogelsang's hypothesis by suggesting that Luther's "Tower experience" (Prenter ably defended this description of Luther's breakthrough, which had been in danger of being too easily abandoned) took place before any of Luther's courses of lectures as a Professor, i.e., when he was first a Doctor of Theology in 1512. He shows powerfully, and I think convincingly, how desperate it is to dismiss Luther's amazing lectures on *Psalms* as entirely within the Catholic sphere—still more Luther's lectures on *Romans* which followed. Doubtless Bizer's and Prenter's studies will soon be translated into English; and with the new materials available the interested reader can follow the debate with reference to the primary documents and reach his own conclusions. My own conviction is that the breakthrough must certainly have occurred before 1515, that is, before Luther's lectures on *Romans*. I cannot believe that this fine and powerful commentary could have been the work of one prevented from entering the Pauline world by theological (and emotional) difficulties about the concept which is the very heart of the epistle. However, there are still problems to be settled, and for me one of the signs that the mystery is still far from being solved is its treatment as a problem of the relation of justification to the Word (Bizer) or of *Justitia* to *misericordia* (Prenter), whereas for Luther the tension is evidently within the very concept of *Justitia*, Righteousness itself. And one cannot but be a little suspicious of the new methodology which seems to be reading back into the evidence the hardened theological categories of later (perhaps the latest) Protestant theology. Prenter is surely right in concluding that "Luther was not a modern theologian—he was a witness to the Gospel."

Luther studies, it can be seen, are very much alive, and the sources are now available which will enable the English reader to follow the recent developments and, if not to probe them to the uttermost detail, to keep on them the kind of check which, in historical studies and in theological questions, the general student has the right to exercise over the specialist. In a world like our own, which needs all the giant voices of its past, it is surely greatly to the benefit of all the churches that this man, Martin Luther, should speak anew to us, in a language comprehensible to all.

GORDON RUPP

University of Manchester
March, 1964

INTRODUCTION

WHO WAS MARTIN LUTHER? What was he really like? If we had
met him, what would have been our personal impression?
Should we have said, 'Ah, yes, a very great man! Did you notice
those eyes?' Or should we have murmured, 'After all, a very dis-
appointing fellow!'? Not all our historical investigation can
bring us there. When the last word has been written, we shall
see Luther through a glass darkly, and what we behold will lack
something which in the days of his too, too solid flesh was per-
ceptible by some unlettered oaf who gaped at him in the streets
of Wittenberg, or by some child who stared back at him along
the lanes of Worms. But we cannot summon Luther from the
vasty deep (or the Elysian fields) as those other alumni of
Wittenberg, Prince Hamlet and Dr. Faustus, were enabled to
view the dead. Nevertheless, we need not surrender to scepticism,
we may pursue with good heart the search for the historical
Luther.

Curiosity seems a vulgar motive for writing history, if not for
reading it, yet this essay results from an attempt to find a
personally satisfying answer to the question, 'Who was Martin
Luther?' I have tried to concentrate on a positive presentation.
One learns that the most elderly and grubby libels continue to
circulate long after they have been met at the exact level of
scholarship, and there is comfort in the knowledge that Luther
is beyond gunshot of them all. I have not tried to impress or
convert those to whom Luther must always be the Enemy
(resembling Mussolini in the famous cartoon, 'The Man who
Took the Lid Off!') Sooner or later even polemical publicists
will tire of re-hashing Denifle and Grisar, and will turn to the
sobrieties of modern Catholic scholars like Kiefl, Joseph Lortz
and Dr. Hessen-Köln.

The great discoveries and most exciting monographs of the
last thirty years of Luther studies have concentrated on 'The
Young Luther', and it is here that for English readers the tale
must be told anew. The older English material is still of value:
J. A. Froude, T. M. Lindsay, Charles Beard knew how to write

and are still to be profitably studied. But much has been written even since the publication of Dr. Mackinnon's four volumes, and we are now better placed to understand Luther's theology, in the context of the ecumenical conversation and of Biblical theology. Whatever the truth about Luther, it will never be found by those who by-pass his theology, though the theologians may deserve also a reminder of the importance of that historical context without which the theological development is but half explained.

The truth about one of the greatest Germans may be of value for the healing of the nations. The truth about the greatest Lutheran must concern the mending of the Church. There is a Luther about whom the Germans and the Lutherans have most right to speak. That does not absolve the rest of us from trying to understand him too. I hope this little book may persuade some to adventure the intricate but richly rewarding field of Luther studies. Getting books from Germany in these post-war days is a highly skilled mystery, and I am grateful to Professors Iwand, Ernst Wolf and H. Bornkamm for the loan of books, to Dr. Wunderlich of the Methodist Seminary in Frankfurt, and to Horst Flachsmeier for seeking volumes otherwise inaccessible. Nearer home, I have to thank Dr. R. N. Flew, Dr. Williams' Library, and the unfailing courtesy and helpfulness of the London Library. A short sketch must beg many questions, but I hope to deal with some of them in more extended studies to be published later.

GORDON RUPP

Richmond College
Surrey
All Saints' Eve, 1949

ABBREVIATIONS

The following abbreviations are used throughout:—

WA   *Works of Luther* (Weimarer Ausgabe).

WA Br   *Letters of Luther*
                 (Weimarer Ausgabe. Briefwechsel).

TR   *Table Talk* (Weimarer Ausgabe. Tischreden).

WML   *Works of Luther* (Philadelphia Edition).

CHAPTER ONE

YOUNG LUTHER

'. . . the man put his fingers in his ears, and ran on crying
Life! Life! Eternal Life! So he looked not behind him, but
fled towards the middle of the Plain.'

'I WAS BORN at Eisleben, and baptized in St. Peter's there. I do not remember this, but I believe my parents and fellow countrymen.'[1] Thus, with characteristic irony, Luther described his origin. He was born November 10th, 1483, to Hans and Margaret (*née* Lindemann)[2] Luther. If the portraits of Cranach are reliable, Martin grew to resemble his father in frame, his mother in eyes and mouth. His parents came from Mohra, on the edge of the Thuringian forest, and he described himself as a 'tough Saxon' of peasant stock.[3] There was always something of the peasant about him, and the texture of his mind was of a plain, honest grain. He could sum up an Italian diplomat as shrewdly as his kinsmen a huckster at the fair, and he had a peasant mixture of common sense and credulity. If he could be vulgar, he had none of the obscenities of the politely learned. Of avarice, in a venal age, he had not the faintest trace.

Hans Luther had ideas of his own, or maybe he was forced to leave Möhra by the pressure of laws of inheritance which, in that fairytale land of towers and gables, seemed most concerned to reward the youngest son. He moved to Eisleben and thence to Mansfeld, to work in the copper mines where it was hard, but the industry was thriving and there were hopes of getting a degree of independence.[4] He hewed to such effect that he was soon able to rent several furnaces, and in 1491 was numbered among the councillors of the little town. (His brother, also Hans

[1] WA Br.1.610.18 (January 14th, 1520).
[2] Boehmer, *Der Junge Luther* (ed. Bornkamm) 1939, p. 358. We cite from this, and from the American translation, *Road to Reformation*, Philadelphia 1946.
[3] TR 5.255.10. 5.558.13. Other references, WA 58.i.2 ff.
[4] W. Andreas, *Deutschland vor der Reformation*, Stuttgart 1948, p. 322.

Luther, was well known to the Bench in a less reputable connection.)

The whole of Luther's life was spent in Saxony, in the triangle of a few thousand square miles, now within the Russian Zone. Saxony was ruled by the House of Wettin, and at the end of the fifteenth century had been divided into Electoral and Ducal Saxony. It sounds simple, but in fact it is symptomatic of the territorial disintegration into which Germany had fallen and which has bedevilled all its subsequent history, the division of jurisdiction between innumerable authorities, 'all the more bewildering that most of them appeared to be composed of patches lying separate from each other. Almost every ruling prince had to cross some neighbour's land to visit the outlying portions of his dominions'.[1]

There are a few anecdotes about Luther's childhood, and they seem fairly reliable. That Margaret Luther might be seen bowed under the weight of the wood she was dragging home from the forest, no more argues extreme poverty than the similar sights to be seen round Berlin in 1947, though both remind us that life in the sixteenth century was nearer the edge of things, to the elemental facts of hunger, thirst, pain and death, than we can easily imagine.

If Luther's recollections of childhood are sombre, it is perhaps because the young have long memories for injustice: if he never forgot that his mother thrashed him until he bled, for taking a nut, and if at school he got fifteen of the best for muddling a declension he had never been told to learn, there have been overstrained mothers and badly trained teachers in other times, and the sixteenth century had its own stern ideas about discipline. Apart from these, and the glimpse of a very small Martin Luther swaying joyously on the shoulders of his big friend, Nicholas Oemler, as he was carried to school, we have to imagine the world of sunshine and shrill laughter and shouting companionship which, we must believe, existed also.[2]

At seven he was sent to the Latin school at Mansfeld, and at fourteen to the city of Magdeburg, perhaps to the Choir School, certainly to receive instruction from the famous fraternity of the

[1] A. D. Lindsay, *History of the Reformation*, 1906, p. 35.
[2] O. Scheel, *M. Luther*, Tübingen 1921, i, p. 32.

Common Life.[1] He made his first acquaintance with the bustle
of an ecclesiastical city, and an indelible impression was made
upon him by the sight of Prince William of Anhalt-Zerbst, who
had turned Franciscan and could be seen with his sack, gaunt,
intense, emaciated, 'so that he looked like a dead man, sheer
skin and bone',[2] as he begged through the streets. After a year,
Luther went to Eisenach where he had kin and where he made
new friends, including Johann Braun, Vicar of St. Mary's. At
Eisenach and Magdeburg he went on frequent carol-singing
expeditions, one of the milder forms of adolescent intimidation,
and long afterwards he loved to tell how he and his friends ran
as a door opened and a loud voice roared gruffly, 'Where are
you, you young ruffians?'—to return shamefaced when it became
plain that the owner of the voice was offering them some sausage!
The terrifying figure, half seen against the surrounding dark,
whose voice of wrath was a mask for kindness, became for
Luther a parable which summed up a deal of his theology.[3]

Hans Luther and his wife must have pondered the problem
of what to do with their gifted son, and the direction of their
thought can be inferred from the fact that in April, 1501,
'Martinus Ludher ex Mansfeld' matriculated in the faculty of
Arts, at the University of Erfurt. Erfurt was a renowned university, one of the oldest (1397) and best attended in Germany,
and early known as a centre of international study (*studium
generale*).[4] At this time its faculty of Law was notable, and
Martin may have gone there rather than to Leipzig because he
was destined for the Law. Though in Saxony, Erfurt came
under the jurisdiction of the Archbishop of Mainz. A fair city,
of perhaps 30,000 inhabitants, well known for its gardens and
gardeners,[5] if its morals left a good deal to be desired, and if
relations between town and gown were in constant tension, the
same could be said of a good many other university towns.

Luther had bed and board at the student hostel of St. George,
and he made friends, talked a good deal (they nicknamed him
'the philosopher') and learned to play the lute. He took the usual

[1] Scheel, i, p. 67; Mackinnon, *Luther*, 1925, i, p. 14; W. J. Kooiman,
Maarten Luther, Amsterdam 1948, p. 11 ff.
[2] WA 38.105.
[3] WA 58.i.3 for many references.
[4] Rashdall, *Mediæval Universities*, 1936, i, p. 7; iii, p. 334.
[5] Andreas, *Deutschland vor der Reformation*, p. 342.

Arts course and proceeded to the Bachelor's degree in 1502.[1] The so-called *trivium* (grammar, logic and rhetoric) may have become arid, but to learn that words have precise meanings, that their right assembly is important and that clear expression determines intelligibility, these 'lost tools of learning' would seem a basis for liberal education for lack of which a good many modern substitutes have gone awry.[2]

Erfurt was a citadel of the latest form of mediæval philosophy, that of the 'modern way' (*via moderna*), the Nominalists. In its late mediæval form it had been launched by William of Occam (1300?–1349) as a rigorous critical antidote to the age of synthesis which had found its thirteenth-century norm in St. Thomas Aquinas.[3] The Nominalist teachers at Erfurt were Jodocus Trutvetter and Bartholomew Arnoldi of Usingen, and under them Luther studied the *quadrivium* (geometry, mathematics, music, astronomy) and the natural, metaphysical and moral philosophy of Aristotle. At the age of twenty-two Luther took his M.A., placed second among seventeen candidates. In an age when only a small proportion of those who went up proceeded as far as the Master's degree, Luther had done all that his parents could have hoped.

For a youth in his position, having respect to the resources and station of his parents, there were two possibilities—lawyer or parson? It may be that the sturdy anti-clericalism which Hans Luther shared with many of his class and age was decisive. Hans Luther paid for a new copy of the *Corpus Juris* and Martin was entered in the faculty of Law. He might one day make a name for himself in Saxony as public notary of Eisleben or Eisenach, or he might achieve the dignity of an official at the court of the Elector Frederick. Then, to crown all, he might win the hand of a mayor's daughter, or the young widow of a merchant of standing![4] Such elevated hopes, we may suppose, were in his father's heart. It might very easily have fallen out

---

[1] Scheel, i, pp. 170–215; Mackinnon, i, pp. 17–27.
[2] D. L. Sayers, *The Lost Tools of Learning*, 1948.
[3] Nominalism began in the age of Abelard (twelfth century). The *via moderna* was concerned with more than the problem of the nature of Universals. M. H. Carré. Realists and Nominalists. *Dict. Théol. Cath.*, xi, articles 'Nominalisme', 'Occam' (P. Vignaux).
[4] WA 8 (*De Votis Monasticis*, 1521) 573.24. 'You planned for me a respectable and wealthy marriage.'

that way, and if it had, the name of Martin Luther might have been known to history from the recondite archives of a little German town. Suddenly all these thoughts were thrown into confusion. To his dismay, mortification and rage, Hans Luther learned that the son for whom he hoped so much, who had but recently been home, talking eagerly about his music and his literary friends, had decided to enter religion and was seeking admission to the monastery of the Austin Friars in Erfurt.

What underlay this fateful decision, so sudden and unexpected that Luther did not inform his father until it had been made?[1]

The evidence is confused, and when we consider that Luther's close friends, Melanchthon and Justas Jonas gave different and irreconcilable versions of the story,[2] we may suspect a reticence on Luther's part which does not exactly tally with the stories in the *Table Talk*.

There are two pieces of primary and authentic evidence. The first is a letter to Luther (October 31st, 1519) from his former fellow student Crotus Rubeanus, now a humanist of high repute, a letter written in the flowery rhetoric of the humanist circle:

Go on, as you have begun! Leave an example to posterity. For you do this not without the divine power. For divine providence had an eye to this when, returning from your parents, celestial lightning flung you to the ground, like another Paul, before the town of Erfurt, and compelled your most doleful severance from our company, within the Augustinian walls.[3]

The other statement is from Luther, in the open letter to his father which prefaced the tract *Concerning Monastic Vows* (1521):

I remember, when you had calmed down, and were talking with me, that I asserted that I had been called by heavenly terrors [*de coelo terroribus*], for not freely or desirously did I become a monk, much less to gratify my belly, but walled around with the terror and agony of sudden death [*terrore et agone mortis subitæ circumvallatus*] I vowed a constrained and necessary vow.[4]

---

[1] 'I did it without telling you, and against your will.' WA 8.573.19.
[2] Melanchthon mentions the death of a friend, and Jonas a vague story of how Luther was on his way home from Gotha when 'there came to him a terrifying apparition from heaven which he at that time interpreted to mean that he should become a monk'. Mackinnon, i, pp. 33 f.; Scheel, i, pp. 321 ff.
[3] WA Br.1.543.105.
[4] WA 8.573.30.

The two passages are generally regarded as confirming the story in the *Table Talk*[1] according to which, on July 2nd, 1505, Luther was returning from a visit to his parents when he was overtaken by a thunderstorm near the village of Stotternheim, not far from Erfurt. In terror, Luther cried, 'Help, St. Anne, and I'll become a monk!' It may be true. St. Anne's was the popular cult, not least among the miners, and she was patroness of a Brotherhood closely connected with the Austin Friars of Erfurt. If Luther considered himself pursued by the thunderbolts of an angry God, the story is possible.

When we ask what did happen, there is confusion, and later versions of the story have been affected by the account given in Luther's *Monastic Vows*, and no doubt, too, by the edifying parallel of the sudden conversion of St. Paul.[2] But how did it happen? Luther might have been severely shaken by a near miss. But it would be all over in a moment, and by the time he could think clearly and had felt himself all over, the natural reaction would surely be relief and not panic-stricken fear of another stroke of lightning such as to evoke this drastic vow? If he was not stricken, we must suppose he felt himself pursued by the anger of God. But we cannot press the point,[3] though another incident in the *Table Talk* deserves to be remembered.

In this, Luther was on a journey home, when he fell and the short dagger which he wore struck deep into his leg, severing an artery. His companion set off to Erfurt for help, and while he was gone Luther tried to staunch the swift bleeding. In peril of death he cried 'Help, Mary!' A surgeon came and Luther was carried to Erfurt.[4] In the night the wound broke open afresh and he again called out to the Virgin. The date assigned in the *Table Talk* is April 16th, 1503, and the place a different road.[4] But there are some striking similarities between the stories, bearing in mind the vagueness of the thunderstorm account, and allowing for the influence of the story of St. Paul. Certainly,

[1] TR 4.4707.
[2] Dr. Nathin said (according to report) that Luther had been 'wonderfully converted through Christ, like another Paul'. Scheel, ii, p. 10.
[3] In favour of the thunderstorm story is WA 44.598.39: 'If a man were struck by divine lightning he would feel his conscience labour vehemently, stripped of all consolation, nor would it easily be assuaged.'
[4] TR 1.119. Scheel, i.320.20. According to Scheel, Biereye in a special study of the problem suggests March 25th, 1505, for this, along the same road as the thunderstorm.

Luther alone, bleeding to death, would be 'walled around by the agony and fear of sudden death' and surrounded by 'heavenly terrors' in such a way as to make a desperate vow intelligible.

If both stories are true, then the crisis of a serious accident may have suggested reflections to Luther which recurred sharply when, a little later, he again faced the imminence of death. The death of a friend, which Melanchthon reports, and which finds some confirmation in the Wittenberg archives, may have deepened such serious consideration. But about the inward state of his mind, there is no real evidence.[1] So Martin Luther sold his books, keeping back his Virgil and his Plautus, and on July 16th, 1505, he had a farewell meal with his friends. The following day he greeted them with, 'To-day you see me, and then, never again', and the sober little group approached the Augustinian monastery.[2] Clutching his bundle, he turned away from them as the gates closed behind him. Within, he was embraced, and entered a new world.

In turning Austin Friar, or, more properly, becoming a member of the Reformed Congregation of the Eremetical Order of St. Augustine, Luther had joined an order of considerable importance, not only in Erfurt. Incorporated by Innocent IV in 1243, confirmed by Alexander IV in 1256, the mendicant order of Augustinian Friars had over two thousand chapters by the middle of the fifteenth century. In 1473 Andreas Proles carried through a reform of the order, and the house at Erfurt was numbered among those Observant houses which accepted a strict interpretation of their Rule, with Proles as Vicar-General. Under his successor, Johannes Staupitz, a revised constitution was made in 1504.[3]

About Luther's monastic career as a whole we have his own abundant testimony in after years. True, the integrity and accuracy of this has often been called in question, notably by Denifle, who declared it to be a deliberate and lying invention which Luther only dared ventilate when those who could contradict him had passed from the scene. But the modern

[1] WA Br.2.384.80 (September 9th, 1521) to Melanchthon: 'I was more snatched than drawn towards it' (*magis fui raptus quam tractus*).

[2] 'Then they led me with tears,' TR 4.4707. Scheel, i, p. 257. For a full discussion of Luther's vocation, see Scheel, i, chap. 5, and notes *ad loc*.

[3] Preserved Smith, *Luther*, London 1911, p. 8; Scheel, i, p. 256.

Catholic historian, Joseph Lortz, declared this 'moral depravity' theory to be a complete failure.[1]

In fact there is independent testimony to Luther's integrity at a much later date than the theory of Denifle could sustain. In 1543 Matthew Flaccius Illyricus reported a conversation with a former companion of the Reformer who had remained a Catholic and who 'declared that Martin Luther lived a holy life among them, kept the Rule most exactly, and studied diligently'.[2]

It may be, as Scheel suggests, that traces of the later 'Luther legend' can be found in stories in the *Table Talk* of the jealousy of other monks, which led them to give Luther menial tasks and sent him out ('Sack on your back, you!') on begging expeditions.[3] On the other hand Luther was greatly gifted, he was zealous, and the prodigious mental activity of his later life must have had some anticipation. But during the period of his novitiate Luther must have been fully occupied learning the etiquette of conventual discipline, the duties of prayer and choir. Of the Master of the Novices he spoke with great affection in later years.

Luther made his profession, with its serious and irrevocable vows, in September, 1506, and was then prepared for ordination (about half the seventy members of the house were priests). He was ordained Sub-Deacon, December, 1506; Deacon, February, 1507; Priest, April, 1507.[4] The first Mass, a great occasion, took place at the beginning of May, and to it Luther invited friends, including his old friend Johann Braun from Eisenach. Second only to the solemnity itself, however, was the reunion with his father. Hans Luther had at first addressed his son with cold and formal displeasure, but others in the home had given softening counsel, and then two sons died of the plague and perhaps it did not take so much after all to reconcile Hans Luther to the boy of whom he must always be proud, however distasteful the thought of his unwelcome calling. Having decided to go, Father Luther

---

[1] H. Strohl, *L'Evolution religieuse de Luther*, Strasbourg, pp. 12 ff.; E. G. Rupp, *Luther: the Catholic Caricature;* Theology, Oct., 1942, references *ad loc.;* J. Lortz, *Reformation in Deutschland*, 1947; G. Miegge, *Lutero*, Torre Pellice 1946, pp. 71 ff.

[2] Scheel, ii, p. 10 *n.*

[3] 'They were jealous of me on account of my study, saying "What's good enough for me is good enough for you. Sack on your back, you" ' (*saccum per naccum*). TR 5.452.34; TR 3.580.5; TR 5.99.24; Scheel, pp. 599 ff.

[4] Following Scheel, Boehmer, Miegge.

did the thing handsomely, sent a generous sum towards the celebration, and rode up with a cavalcade of twenty. Martin took the first opportunity to explain the imperious nature of his vocation, to which his father, with great effort to keep his temper, grunted, 'Let's hope it wasn't all imagination'.[1] But the undercurrent was there, and his indignation exploded on the company when across the table and amid an embarrassed silence he asked loudly, 'Have you not read in Scripture that one shall honour one's father and mother?' To Martin Luther the words struck deeply home.

In reading for ordination, Luther studied the treatise on the Canon of the Mass by the famous Tübingen preacher and Nominalist theologian, Gabriel Biel (d. 1495). Thus he approached the sacred rite with an overwhelming sense of the Divine Majesty, and of the dreadful prerogative vouchsafed to one who was commissioned to intercede with the Living God.[2]

The Augustinians at Erfurt had close association with the University, and Luther was selected as apt for advanced theological study. Under Johann Paltz (who left in 1507) and Johann Nathin (a former student under Biel) Luther imbibed the doctrines of the *via moderna* as refracted through Biel and his own preceptors.

The nature and extent of Luther's debt to Occamism cannot be clarified in the present state of studies of late scholasticism.[3] Many of Luther's apparently deferential remarks about Occam prove to be ironical.[4] Luther's first onslaught on tradition was directed against an Aristotelianism as marked in Occam as in Scotus or Aquinas. When the theological controversy opened, it was the Nominalist doctrine of human nature which was the centre of Luther's attack. There is no evidence that Luther was influenced by Occam's anti-papal writings, and Biel, the more immediate influence upon him, is hailed by Catholic scholars as impeccable in his attitude to Rome.[5]

[1] WA 8.574.2: 'Would (you said) that it may not have been an illusion or phantasy.' Cf. K. Holl, *Gesammelte Aufsätze. Luther*, Tübingen 1927, p. 15, *n*. 1.

[2] The stories of Luther's attempt to flee from the altar are so riddled with confusion that in the light of Scheel's discussion (ii, pp. 97–109), accepted by Mackinnon (i.46) and Miegge (47) they can be dismissed.

[3] See the remarks of P. Vignaux (*Dict. Théol. Cath.*, xi, pp. 717, 876). Since then (1931) there has been some improvement.

[4] K. Holl, *Ges. Aufs. Luther*, p. 49, *n*. 2; TR 2.516.6; WA 30.ii.300.9.

[5] C. Rich, *Dict. Théol. Cath.*, ii, pp. 814–25.

This is not at all to deny the influence of the *via moderna* upon Luther. It was the one form of scholasticism which he knew intimately, for we misunderstand entirely if we suppose late mediæval German Catholic theology to be dominated by Thomism: in many places the struggle for the future must have seemed to lie between Scotus and Occam. Never before or since have Germans been so preoccupied with, or so respectful to, British theology![1]

Occam bequeathed his followers a tradition of logical, critical enquiry which was bound to influence those who used the dialectical weapon. To the end of his life, Luther kept a partiality for the syllogism, and for illustrations drawn from logic and from grammar. As regards the problem of Universals, Luther repeatedly affirmed himself a Nominalist.[2] There is continuity as well as discontinuity in Luther's thought. P. Vignaux has suggested that in his disputations on the Trinity (1543-5) Luther used arguments already to be found in his marginal notes of 1509.[3] The rigorous and sustained argument of his 'Bondage of the Will' (1525) against Erasmus, and 'Of the Lord's Supper' (1528) against Zwingli, are not, as his opponents gibed, an inconsistent relapse into scholasticism, but are rather the full deployment of theological resources which he never repudiated, for despite his attack upon it, Luther had more respect for scholastic theology than Erasmus or Zwingli.

Recent studies upon Occam[4] have counselled caution about the generalizations of the older historians of dogma, in regard to the alleged Occamist 'Voluntarism', the stress on the Divine Will, the sharp division which, it is claimed, the Occamists interposed between reason and revelation.

[1] It is refreshing to find that Luther thinks of the English rather than the French as the logical people. TR 5.649.26: 'Scotus, Occam, were English. The French could never produce people like that!'

[2] TR 5.653. WA 39.ii.11.36.

[3] P. Vignaux, *Luther. Commentateur des Sentences*, Paris 1935, pp. 25, 29; WA 39.ii.253, WA ix.31.31.

[4] E. A. Moody, *Logic of William of Ockham*, London 1935; E. Guelluy, *Philosophie et Theologie chez Ockham*, Paris 1947; *The Tractatus de Predestinatione ... of Wm. of Ockham* (Ph. Boehner) New York 1945; E. Gilson, *La Philosophie au Moyen Age*, Paris 1930, chap. xi; G. De Lagarde, *Naissance de l'esprit laïque au déclin du Moyen Age*, Paris 1942-46, iv-vi; *Wm. of Ockham. Dict. Théol. Cath.* articles, 'Nominalisme', 'Occam' (P. Vignaux); P. Vignaux, *Justification et Predestination au XIV siecle*, Paris 1934, *Luther, Commentateur des Sentences*, Paris 1935.

We are better placed in the light of recent detailed study to see the positive Occamist concern for the Liberty of God (against the doctrines of necessity in Pelagius, and Peter of Auriol, and, in the case of Biel, as against a fellow Nominalist, Gregory of Rimini), the refusal to entangle God in his own systems, and the stress on the Divine mercy. We have learned not to make Occam too modern, for he worked with the mediæval ingredients, Scripture and Fathers as focussed in Peter Lombard, Augustine and Aristotle, and he puts his most daring expositions forward as an interpretation of the authentic Augustine or Aristotle.[1] The Occamist stress on the immediacy of the Divine knowledge and action, and the refusal (as against Scotus) to construct a divine psychology, may also have had some effect on Luther. These influences, however, are of a kind to be reflected in subtle undertones, to be detected by deep and sympathetic study. They are in no wise, as in some recent polemic, to be apprized on the strength of superficial verbal similarities, or on what Milton called 'the ferrets and mouse-hunts of an index'.

Late in 1508 Luther was transferred to Wittenberg, to lecture in the Arts Faculty on the Nichomachean Ethics of Aristotle. It was to be a fateful association, this of Luther's with Wittenberg, but at the time it was drastic and depressing. Wittenberg, with its sandy, inhospitable soil, 'on the edge of beyond', presented a dismal contrast to the gardens of 'many-towered Erfurt', and seemed to struggle to support its two thousand inhabitants without the supererogatory burden of a new university.[2]

But over Wittenberg the Elector Frederick brooded with loving care. To it he was as generous as he could afford to be, though his good intentions did not always filter through the thrifty care of his treasurers, and in the matter of rebuilding, promises tended to fall short of performance. Still, one way and another a good deal of building went on between the Castle, the Castle Church, the monasteries and the town, in a descending order of priorities. Frederick contrived that the Chapter of the Schlosskirche and the two monasteries should bear as much as possible of the charge of the University professorships. Within the Schlosskirche itself he housed an impressive and growing

---

[1] M. H. Carré, *Phases of Thought in England*, 1949, pp. 88–178.
[2] TR 3.2871, TR 4.681.

collection of sacred relics, to which were attached privileges nicely calculated to provide edification to visitors and profit to the citizens. But his special interest was the University, since Leipzig and Erfurt fell within the jurisdiction of his neighbours. The foundation was approved by the Emperor in 1502, and confirmed by the Pope in 1503. Dr. Martin Pollich was appointed the first Rector, and the Dean was to be the Vicar-General of the Saxon Province of the Augustinians, Dr. Johann von Staupitz. The Augustinians provided two teaching Chairs, one in Biblical Theology which was held by Staupitz, the other in Moral Philosophy, to which Luther was now suddenly called. In Wittenberg, Luther had to combine his teaching duties with his own studies, and he found the programme strenuous, the enforced preoccupation with Aristotle increasingly uncongenial. 'The study takes it out of me,' he sighed to Johann Braun, 'especially in philosophy which from the beginning I would gladly have exchanged for theology, I mean that theology which searches out the nut from the shell, the kernel from the grain, and the marrow from the bones.'[1]

Johann von Staupitz was of moment in Luther's life, and their friendship was to endure more than common discouragement, and to persist across a growing divide until the death of the older man. Staupitz (b. 1460?) came of noble family and studied at several universities, all associated with the *via antiqua*. He was at Cologne (1483), Leipzig (1485) and Tubingen (1497), taking his doctorate in 1500. It has been plausibly conjectured that his theological affinities lay between the Thomists and the school of Aegidius Romanus, one of the great doctors of his own order. It would be strongly Augustinian.[2] As Vicar-General of the Saxon Province, Staupitz revised the constitutions of the order as prelude to a programme of reform, supporting the Observant Austin Friars who stood for the primitive integrity of the Rule, as against the more relaxed discipline of the Conventuals, who adhered to the accommodations by which the Rule had been adapted to later circumstances. This business of the Order involved long and frequent journeys, and Staupitz

[1] WA Br.1.17.4: 'Violentum est studium.' 'Violentum' appears to be used in the active sense. I think Boehmer is wrong in referring Luther's desire for the really discriminating theology to his zeal for Occamism.

[2] Scheel, ii, pp. 364 ff.; E. Wolf, *Staupitz und Luther*, Leipzig 1927, pp. 30–35.

must have found it difficult to discharge his University responsibilities. He may have had early thoughts about looking for an eventual successor among the young men. Although most recent historians are against the view, the possibility exists that he had made earlier acquaintance with Luther, had been directly responsible for calling him to further studies and to Wittenberg.

In the following March Luther took the degree of 'Baccalaureus Biblicus' at Wittenberg. He returned to Erfurt for the next rank of Sententiarius and became entangled in a sufficiently modern difficulty of university red tape. Wittenberg was very young, and Erfurt very conscious of its seniority, and so there was an Oxbridge *v*. Redbrick affair of ruffled academic dignity. The thing was to flare up again when Luther would take his doctorate at Wittenberg. Then he recalled how, on this earlier occasion, the Dean, Sigismund Thomae of Stockheim, had been droning drowsily away with lengthy extracts from the University regulations when Dr. Nathin exploded impatiently, waved the Dean aside, and read simply the list of required text-books from a chit of paper in his hand. A lively scene, the point of which is that in the fuss nobody asked Luther to make the regulation promise to take his further degrees and duties at Erfurt![1] As Sententiarius, Luther was required to lecture on the Sentences of Peter Lombard, the great theological text-book of the Middle Ages. We have Luther's notes on them, and on the collection of works of St. Augustine which he read at this time.[2] Hitherto he had not been drawn to St. Augustine,[3] but now he really devoured him with the rapture of a younger theologian for his first theological love, as the enthusiastic marginal comments ('Beautiful! Beautiful!', in striking contrast to the 'Completely mad!' of his later marginal comments on Biel) eloquently witness. This new and headlong enthusiasm for Augustine may account for the ferocity of his note against the Alsatian humanist Wimpfeling, who (in his 'De Integritate' (1505)) had roused

---

[1] WA Br.1.30 (December 21st, 1514), 15–25.

[2] WA ix, pp. 1–94; P. A. Vignaux, *Luther. Commentateur des Sentences;* Holl, *Luther,* pp. 187 ff.

[3] WA Br.1.70.20 (October 19th, 1516): 'Before I fell in with his books, I had very little room for him.' TR 1.140.5: 'In the beginning I devoured Augustine.' Luther had not yet come to know the anti-Pelagian works of Augustine.

the embattled fury of the Augustinians by denying that St. Augustine had ever been a monk.[1]

Though we cannot agree with those who find in these notes the beginning of Luther's doctrine of grace and justification, or the evidence of the theological influence of Staupitz, there is a boldness of judgment and a discrimination between authorities which is remarkable. For the Master of the Sentences, Luther maintained lifelong respect, and it is significant that Peter Lombard represents the twelfth-century combination of Scripture and Fathers on the eve of the great thirteenth-century invasion of Aristotle. In Luther's acid comments in the notes upon Aristotle, there is a discrimination between traditional theology and what P. Vignaux has called the philosophic 'envelope' of Aristotelian scholasticism.[2] Luther's attack on indulgences in 1517 was to be preceded by a public attack on the Aristotelian domination of theology, but here are its beginnings in a positive programme of simplification, the return to what Luther was later (1516) to call 'our theology . . . the Bible, St. Augustine and the old Fathers'. The great humanist attack on scholasticism did not get fully under way until the Reuchlin affair of the next decade, but here in 1509–10 is another programme, different from that which Erasmus was to adumbrate in the return to the 'philosophy of Christ' in the Gospels.

Meanwhile, Staupitz had conjured up a quarrel which cut dangerously across the party line. Seven Observant houses (including Erfurt and Nuremberg) withstood a project to unite all the German congregations, and Luther was told off to assist Dr. Nathin in concerting the opposition. An attempt to win support from the Archbishop of Magdeburg failed, and it was decided that two brothers should take the case to Rome. The senior was probably selected at Nuremberg, and his 'socius itinerarius' was to be Martin Luther. It was to be the longest journey of his life, and since the Eternal City was the goal, he looked forward to it with eager and filial expectancy. It was late in the year 1510 that they set out for the arduous crossing of the Alps and the descent into the Lombard plain. We have only a few anecdotes in later years about the journey. There is the vivid story of how the two brethren slept on one occasion with

---

[1] WA ix.12.7.
[2] See P. Vignaux, *Luther, Commentateur*, p. 24.

their windows open to the Italian mists, with dire results, so that for one day they could only crawl miserably along, parched with thirst for water too dirty to drink, and nauseated by the sickly wine, until the gift of two pomegranates relieved them, and as they munched noisily, cheerfulness broke in.[1] When Luther came in sight of Rome, he dropped to the ground with a pious 'Hail, holy Rome!'[2] Their business broached to the authorities, the two travellers made the customary tour of churches and of catacombs, drinking in the manifold and edifying marvels. The Italian cities must have been intriguing, and Rome, twice the size of Erfurt and, despite the absence of Pope and court, an emotional climax of bustle, swagger and Italian panache, great buildings, churches innumerable, and acres and acres of unintelligible and reverend ruins. Luther was disgusted by the Roman clergy with their slick and cynical professionalism, as they murmured their devotions at high speed, nudging him angrily with *'Passa, Passa!* Get a move on, you!' The story that on the stairs of the Scala Sancta Luther heard a premonition of his later gospel is a fable,[3] though there may be the germ of truth in the story that at this point he wondered 'Who knows whether all this is true?' Luther was simple enough, and good enough, to be deeply shocked by some of the things he saw, by the living proof of the tales of vice and luxury, covetousness and degradation in high places. 'I would never have believed that the Papacy was such an abomination, if I had not myself seen the Roman court.'[4]

Homesick, the two travellers found friends among the members of the German Church in Rome, and they patriotically agreed that this was the best of all the Roman churches.[5] The appeal to Rome was a failure, and perhaps Luther himself became convinced of the weakness of the cause, for on his return to Germany he no longer supported the opposition to Staupitz and he and his friend John Lang won a good deal of unpopularity from their Erfurt brethren. Staupitz was impressed by Luther, and, as we shall see, not a little concerned about

[1] TR 4.4104.
[2] TR 5.467.13.
[3] It is a pity that it was accepted by Dr. N. P. Williams (*Ideas of the Fall and Original Sin*, London 1927, p. 426).
[4] WA 47.432.28.
[5] WA 47.425.5.

him. He decided that Luther must proceed to the doctorate and succeed him in the Chair of Biblical Theology at Wittenberg.

Although this was the logical climax of his academic training, Luther shrank from it. He told later how under a pear tree in the garden he discussed the matter with Staupitz, pleading (perhaps only half seriously) his own expectancy of an early death, until Staupitz joked his objections aside and commanded him to the new step as a matter of obedience. To become a Doctor in Theology meant much more than to take a higher degree: it committed the graduate to a life of public teaching, and to a life of preaching, from which also Luther may have drawn back. The minor question arose, whence would come the not inconsiderable expenses for the occasion, and this was solved, on the petition of Staupitz, by the thrifty generosity of the Elector. It seems likely that it was contrived that the Elector should hear Luther preach, but what settled the matter was the assurance that Luther would succeed Staupitz in the Chair of Theology. On October 19th, 1512, with the rich, solemn proprieties which inaugurated a Doctor in Theology, Luther was invested with his new calling. 'Calling' it was for him, not only in the mediæval sense of an *officium*, but in the important sense of his own later doctrine of the Christian life. In this moment, Luther became a public as well as a private person, solemnly called upon to defend the Word of God and to drive away all erroneous and strange doctrines, and the compulsion of this calling was to sustain his courage in many difficult hours.

So once again it seemed that the lines of Luther's career were settled. At the age of twenty-eight he was a Doctor of Divinity and a Professor of Sacred Theology, with some sort of understanding made over his head[1] that he would spend the rest of his days in Wittenberg. It all seems rather final for a young man, this settled prospect of a long succession of interesting but uneventful years, a narrow horizon bounded by disputations, lectures, and academic gossip. In one sense it was just that. We shall never understand Luther unless we remember that he was by trade a Theological Professor, that year in, year out (the exceptions can be counted on the fingers), twice a week at the

---

[1] 'Martin should discharge for the rest of his life the lectureship at Wittenberg pertaining to him' (Staupitz). Scheel, ii, p. 556.

appointed hour, he walked into the lecture-room and addressed successive generations of students, and this for thirty years until he was old and feeble and could only croak his last lecture.[1] This was the career which opened for Martin Luther in 1512. In between lectures, so to speak, he attended the deathbed of a world and assisted the birth of a new age.

[1] H. Boehmer, *Luther's Erste Vorlesung*, Leipzig 1924; H. Bornkamm, *Luther und das Alte Testament*, Tübingen 1948, p. 6.

CHAPTER TWO

MR. FEARING

'When we came at the Hill Difficulty, he made no stick at that, nor did he much fear the lions: for you must know that his trouble was not about such things as those: his fear was about his acceptance at last.'

WHETHER LUTHER'S ENTRY into the monastery was as abrupt as it seems, or as Holl suggested, 'the fulfilment of a secret wish',[1] has been much debated. Luther's own words, 'Walled around with the terror and agony of sudden death', remind us that it was the prospect of death, and death not so much as physical dissolution but as the door to judgment, which moved him. In the cover of his copy of Augustine's *City of God* there is written, in Luther's hand, the quotation from the *Phædo* of Plato, '*Divinus Plato: Philosophia esti melete thanatos*' ('Philosophy is the study of death'), and as P. Vignaux comments, sometimes a very personal experience may underly a classical quotation.[2] There are very few periods in Luther's life when he did not feel death to be an imminent possibility, and it may have been more in earnest than in jest that he put this to Staupitz as a reason why he should not proceed to his doctorate.

In contrast was the assurance given Luther at his profession: 'Keep this Rule, and I promise you eternal life.'[3]

He sought evangelical perfection with earnest and strenuous zeal, and with that wholeheartedness which was the quality of all his undertakings: 'I had no other thoughts, but to keep my Rule.'[4] In 1533 he could say, 'I was a good monk, and kept strictly to my order, so that I could say that if the monastic life could get a man to heaven, I should have entered: all my companions who knew me would bear witness to that.'[5] The Master of the Novices gave him the *Lives of the Fathers*, and for a time

---

[1] K. Holl, *Luther*, p. 15. [2] P. Vignaux, *Luther, Commentateur*, p. 13.
[3] WA 51.83.8, 40.i.244.7. [4] WA 47.92.10, 40.ii.15.15, 43.255.9.
[5] WA 38.143.25.

his head was stuffed full of devout fancies about the desert hermits. 'I used to imagine such a saint, who would live in the desert, and abstain from food and drink, and live on a few vegetables and roots and cold water.'[1] He exercised himself in austerities to the point of danger. 'I vexed myself with fasts and prayers beyond what was common,[2] and he said later, 'If I could have got to heaven by fasting, I should have merited that twenty years ago.'[3]

At first things went well: 'I know from my own experience, and that of many others, how peaceful and quiet Satan is accustomed to be in one's first years as a priest or monk.'[4] Then, trouble began. They were not 'carnal temptations' of a physical kind, for Luther, though not wood or stone, did not find them cause of racking torment, and he marvelled that St. Jerome should have been thus harassed, while he himself was vexed, 'not about women, but about the really knotty problems.'[5] Even as an adolescent, Luther had made his confession with more than common exactitude,[6] and now, confronted with the goal of perfection, the divine imperative became something which withered all joy, and brought him a torment of doubt and uncertainty and guilt, an inner scepticism which ate corrosively through all the offices of consolation which were offered him. 'When I was a monk, I tried with all diligence to live according to the Rule, and I used to be contrite, to confess and number off my sins, and often repeated my confession, and sedulously performed my allotted penance. And yet my conscience could never give me certainty, but I always doubted and said, "You did not perform that correctly. You were not contrite enough. You left that out of your confession." The more I tried to remedy an uncertain, weak and afflicted conscience with the traditions of men, the more each day found it more uncertain, weaker, more troubled.'[7] 'After watchings, studies, fastings, prayers and other most severe exercises with which as a monk I afflicted myself almost to death, yet that doubt was left in the soul, and I thought "Who knows whether such things are pleasing to God?" '[8]

He tried mental prayer and contemplation, and fancied himself

---

[1] WA 40.ii.103.12. [2] WA 40.ii.574.8. [3] WA 40.ii.453.8.
[4] WA 8.660.31. [5] TR 1.240.12, TR 1.47.15. [6] TR 1.200.26.
[7] WA 40.ii.15.15, WA 40.i.615.6, WA 26.12.12. [8] WA 40.ii.414.15.

among choirs of angels, drove himself nearly daft, as he said, trying to follow the mystic counsels of St. Bonaventura, until his own common sense bade him desist,[1] leaving him permanently suspicious of all who relied on visions and on ecstasies. His spiritual directors were wise and kindly, though even they found their patience[2] tried with what seemed to them just a rather extreme case of 'scruples'.

'Scruples' were a well-known morbid condition of the anxious soul, discussed in a whole literature of moral theology, including treatises by Cassian, William of Paris, Gerson, John Nider and Gabriel Biel, and the symptoms could be recognized as easily as a modern physician can diagnose measles.[3] One method of treating anxious souls was to put their offences in more cheering proportion, and some of the advice given by Gerson is along those lines. There is a type of vanity which loves to parade its own shortcomings, and for such the old rhyme is salutary:

> Once in a saintly passion
> I cried with desperate grief
> 'O Lord, my heart is black with guilt,
> Of Sinners I am chief.'

> Then stooped my guardian angel
> And whispered from behind,
> 'Vanity, my little man!
> You're nothing of the kind!'

But Luther was not to be jokingly fobbed off into a false security which he judged to be one of the dreadful vices of the age:

'Ah!' they say, 'what are you so careful about? It isn't necessary. Just be humble and patient. Do you think God requires such strictness from you? He knows what you are thinking, and He is good. One groan will please him. You imagine that nobody can be saved

---

[1] TR 1.302.30; WA 26.55.17.

[2] TR 1.201.1.

[3] D. Carey, S.J., *The Nature and Treatment of Scruples*, Dublin 1948. There would seem to be specifically Catholic forms of scruples surrounding the sacraments. The Protestant form of the disease was to evoke a casuistry of faith in the seventeenth century, though here there is continuity as well as discontinuity, for we find William Ames transcribing whole passages from William of Paris!

unless he acts so rigidly ... it really is necessary to observe discretion.'
And so gradually the unhappy soul forgets the fear of the Lord, and
that the Kingdom of Heaven suffers violence.[1]

But Luther (it is the measure of his torment) could not forget
the fear of the Lord, and it was his own soul which suffered
violence. That is why he came to choose the word *Anfechtung* for
'temptation', as a description of his spiritual conflict.[2] The full
significance of this word for him can only be discussed in terms
of his developed theology, and he was only to feel the full force
of it in the lonely decisions of what Miegge has called 'his
terrible vocation as a revolutionary'. Yet the spiritual struggles
of his monastic career belong to the same story. They, too, are
Anfechtung.

In the monastery, I did not think about women, or gold, or goods,
but my heart trembled, and doubted how God could be gracious to
me. Then I fell away from faith, and let myself think nothing less
than that I had come under the Wrath of God, whom I must
reconcile with my good works.[3]

What it means to feel oneself under the Wrath of God is
something that modern man can hardly understand. Luther
described the experience in many passages of sombre and com-
pelling beauty, of which the most moving is his exposition of the
flight of Jonah (1526). But in 1518 he describes it in terms which,
if not directly autobiographical, derive power from his own
experience:

I knew a man, who said, that he had often suffered these pains
[infernal torments] in the shortest possible compass of time, so great
and infernal that 'nor tongue nor pen can show' nor can those
believe who have not experienced, so that if they were completed, or
lasted half an hour, or even the tenth part of an hour, he would
utterly perish, and his bones be reduced to ashes. Then God appears
horrifyingly angry and with him, the whole creation. There can be
no flight, no consolation, neither within or without, but all is

---

[1] WA 3.447.21 ff.
[2] Some fine essays have been concerned with this problem, notably G.
Jacob, *Der Gewissensbegriff in der Theologie Luthers*, Tübingen 1929; E. Vogelsang, *Der Angefochtene Christus bei Luther*, Berlin 1932; Y. J. E. Alanen, *Das
Gewissen bei Luther*, Helsinki 1934; L. Pinomaa, *Der Zorn Gottes in der Theologie
Luthers*, Helsinki 1938; P. Buhler, *Die Anfechtung bei Martin Luther*, Zurich,
1942.
[3] WA 47.590.6.

accusation. Then he laments, 'I am cast away from thy face: Lord accuse me not in thy Wrath.' In this moment, marvellous to relate, the soul cannot believe it can ever be redeemed, but that it is suffering a punishment not yet complete, . . . and left only with the naked longing for help, and terrifying trembling, but it knows not whence help can come. This is the soul stretched out with Christ, so that all his bones can be numbered, nor is there any corner not filled with the most bitter bitterness, horror, fear, dolour, but all these things seem eternal. And to use an illustration, it is as though a sphere should pass over a straight line, so that the point of the line which is touched supports the whole sphere, yet does not embrace the whole sphere. So the soul at this point, when it is touched with this passing eternal inundation, feels and drinks nothing less than eternal punishment, but it does not last, for it passes on.[1]

The projection of a wounded conscience on the world outside, with the sense of claustrophobia and agoraphobia, resembles Pip's experiences in *Great Expectations*. 'Instead of my running at everything, everything seemed to run at me. This was very disagreeable to my guilty mind. The gates and dykes and banks came bursting at me through the mist, as if they cried as plainly as could be, "A boy with somebody else's pork pie! Stop him!" '

Here it is, in Luther's recurrent illustration of a 'driven leaf':

Then the conscience feels that all the ill fortune which overtakes it is the Wrath of God, and it thinks that all the creatures are simply God and the Wrath of God, even if it is just a rustling leaf . . . for there is nothing more trivial and insignificant than a dry leaf, which lies on the earth, so that the very insects crawl over it . . . yet when its 'hour' comes, at its rustling shall steed, man, spear, armour, King, Prince, the whole might of an army, and all such proud, bloodthirsty and angry tyrants which otherwise no hell nor yet any Wrath of God, nor judgment can terrify, but only makes them harder and prouder. What fine fellows we are! We are not afraid for any Wrath of God, and we stand upright, and yet we panic and run away from a powerless dry leaf! At such a rustling a leaf becomes the Wrath of God, and the whole world too narrow upon which a little before we strutted upon in our pride.[2]

And, in another place:

Then comes remorse and terrifies the conscience. Then all's right with the world, and he alone is a sinner. God is gracious to all the world save to him alone. Nobody else has to meet God's Wrath save he alone, and he feels there is no wrath anywhere than he feels and he finds himself the most miserable of men. So it was with Adam and Eve when they sinned: had God not come when the cool of the day arrived, they would never have noticed their sin. But when He came, they crept away . . .'[1]

There are those who see in such descriptions only a morbid sensitivity. Yet it is to be noted that those who have attempted a psychological description of Luther's troubles, not only disagree but cancel one another out, while the most impressive of such attempts can only make its diagnosis by abusing evidence in a manner which no historian could countenance, and by making nonsense of Luther's theology.[2]

Luther, says Boehmer, was grateful by temperament, and in later life he again and again recalled the comfort he had received from Staupitz. 'If I didn't praise Staupitz, I should be a damnable, ungrateful, papistical ass . . . for he was my first father in this teaching, and he bore me in Christ. If Staupitz had not helped me out, I should have been swallowed up and left in hell.'[3] To the Nominalist philosophy with its recurring 'perhaps' and its emphasis on the power of the human will, Staupitz brought the wholesome corrective of the *via antiqua*, with its emphasis on the design of God, and the work of grace within the human soul. He brought the mystical emphasis of the 'modern devotion' which found temptation and tribulation to be a sign of grace, a mark of conformity with Christ.

Luther's most illuminating testimony to this help was written in 1518:

I remember, dear Father, that once, among those most pleasant and wholesome talks of thine, with which the Lord Jesus often gives me wondrous consolation, this word 'penitence' [*poenitentia*] was mentioned. We were moved with pity for many consciences, and for those tormentors who teach with rules innumerable and unbearable what they call a 'method of confession'. Then we heard you say, as with a voice from heaven, that there is no true penitence which does not begin with a love of righteousness and of God, and that this love

[1] WA 19.210.14.
[2] Dr. Med. P. J. Reiter, *Martin Luthers Umwelt, Charakter und Psychose*, vol. i, Die Umwelt 1937; vol. ii, *Luther's Persönlichkeit, Seelenleben und Krankheiten*, Copenhagen 1941. The second volume has a useful assembly of evidence.
[3] WA 58.i.27 ff.

which others think to be the completion of penitence is rather its beginning.

This word of yours stuck in me like a 'sharp arrow of the mighty' (Ps. 120, v. 4) and I began from that time onward to compare it with the texts of Scripture which teach penitence. And then began a most joyful game. The words played up to me, smiling agreement and jostling one another on all sides. So that whereas before there was no word more bitter to me than 'penitence' which I feigned sedulously in the presence of God, and sought to express in a forced and fictitious love, now none has to me a more sweet and pleasant sound. For thus the precepts of God grow sweet when we seek not so much to understand them in books, but in the wounds of the most sweet saviour.[1]

Luther goes on to tell how, when he came to study Greek, he found that the authentic meaning of 'penitence' as 'repent' rather than 'do penance', confirmed what Staupitz had told him.

It is possible that Luther's doubts had taken a more desperate turn. The doctrine of Predestination he could not ignore, for it was treated in all the text-books. The torment of his conscience, the anguish which seemed to anticipate infernal pain, was bound to suggest the possibility that he might be numbered among the reprobate. In this problem lay an almost final anguish. As he wrote in 1525:

I myself have more than once been offended [by this doctrine] almost to the very depth and abyss of despair, so that I wished I had never been created a man, until I realized how salutary was this despair and how near to grace.[2]

And when, sometimes, the skies cleared and he had good days, there came the thought that this might be yet a further sign of divine displeasure: 'the greatest temptation is to have no temptation.'[3] We can see how such thoughts choked every attempt of Luther, following scholastic teaching, to make acts of Love to God, and resulted in a constrained and hypocritical devotion, while deep down he felt a murmuring against a God who weighted everything against the sinner, driving him almost to the point of explicit and open blasphemy. But we cannot say when Luther's thoughts about Predestination began to trouble him, or when they reached their most acute tension.

---

[1] WA 1.525.   [2] WA 18.719.7 ff.   [3] WA 3.420.16 ff.

There remains the most important piece of evidence, the autobiographical fragment embedded in Luther's preface to his *Works* (1545). There, after rehearsing his career until the year 1519, he pauses and adds:

Meanwhile, in that year [1519] I turned once more to interpret the Psalms, relying on the fact that I was the more expert after I had handled in the schools the letters of St. Paul to the Romans and Galatians, and that which is to the Hebrews. I had indeed been seized with a great eagerness to understand Paul in the Epistle to the Romans, and, as Virgil says, 'It was not coldness of blood' which held me up, but this one word, that is, in Chap. I. The Justice [*Justitia*] of God is revealed in [the gospel]. For I hated this word 'Justice of God', which by the use and custom of all doctors I had been taught to understand philosophically as they say, as that formal and active justice whereby God is just and punishes unjust sinners.

For, however irreproachable my life as a monk, I felt myself, in the presence of God, to be a sinner with a most unquiet conscience, nor would I believe him to be pleased with my satisfaction. I did not love, indeed I hated this just God who punished sinners, and if not with silent blasphemy, at least with huge murmuring I was indignant against God, as if it were really not enough that miserable sinners, eternally ruined by original sin, should be crushed with every kind of calamity by the law of the Ten Commandments, but God through the Gospel must add sorrow on sorrow, and through the Gospel bring his wrath and justice to bear on us. I raged with a fierce and disturbed conscience in this way, and yet I knocked with importunity at Paul in this place, with a burning desire to know what St. Paul could intend.

At last, God being merciful, as I meditated day and night, pondering the connection of the words, namely, 'The Justice of God is revealed, as it is written, the Just shall live by faith', there I began to understand that Justice of God in which the just man lives by the gift of God, i.e. by faith, and this sentence, 'the Justice of God is revealed in the Gospel' to be understood passively as that whereby the merciful God justifies us by faith, as it is written, 'the just shall live by faith'. At this I felt myself to be born anew, and to enter through open gates into paradise itself. From here, the whole face of the Scriptures was altered. I ran through the Scriptures as memory served, and collected the same analogy in other words as *opus dei*, that which God works in us; *virtus dei*, that in which God makes us strong; *sapientia dei*, in which he makes us wise; *fortitudo dei*, *salus dei*, *gloria dei*.

And now, as much as I formerly hated that word 'Justice of God' [*Justitia Dei*] so now did I love and extol it as the sweetest of all words and then this place was to me as the gates of paradise. Afterwards I read St. Augustine, 'Of the Spirit and the Letter', and beyond all hope, found that he also similarly interpreted the Justice of God as that with which God clothes us and by which we are justified . . . armed with these cogitations I began the second course on the Psalms.[1]

The document involves complicated historical questions which cannot detain us here.[2] But the whole autobiographical fragment has been critically examined by Stracke, and Luther comes out of it surprisingly well.[3]

A long catena of passages can confirm that, in fact, the thought of the 'Justice of God' as retributive punishing justice lay at the heart of Luther's troubles. Thus, in 1515:

If I may speak personally, the word 'justice' nauseated me to hear, so that I should not have been sorry if somebody had made away with me.

And in 1531:

For this the holy fathers who wrote about the Psalms were wont to expound as the 'Just God' as that in which he vindicates and punishes not as that which justifies. So it happened to me as a young man, that I hated this term for God, and even to-day I am as though terrified when I hear God called 'Just'.

Here, Luther's fears congealed. The thought of the severity of God, of Christ as a judge, he had learned from his childhood, and perhaps the sombre mood was reinforced by the strictness of the home.[4] Next, the inexorable demand of the monastic discipline, the goal of evangelical perfection. Then, the Nominalist

[1] WA 54.179–87.
[2] I hope to deal elsewhere with the questions raised by Denifle in his famous 'Die Abendländischen Schriftausleger bis Luther, über Justitia Dei', *Luther und Luthertum*, 2. Aufl. Bd. 1, 2 Abt. Mainz 1905. See the two replies: K. Holl, *Ges. Aufs.* iii, Westen, *Die Justitia Dei in der vorlutherischen Bibelauslegung des Abendlandes;* E. Hirsch, *Initium Theologiæ Lutheri, Festschrift für J. Kaftan* 1920.
[3] Stracke, *Luther's Grosse Selbstzeugnis*, Leipzig 1926.
[4] In a sermon Luther says: 'When such a fear is inbred in a man as a child, it will only with great difficulty be uprooted as long as he lives, for he who trembled at every word of his father or mother, for the rest of his life is afraid of a rustling leaf.' L. Pinomaa, *Zorn Gottes*, p. 153, *n.*

theology with its jargon of merit, the apparently easy-going demand that a man should do 'what within him lies' which led instead to preoccupation with self, to uncertainty and despair, and the increasing tendency to think of salvation in quantitative rather than qualitative terms. So Luther's religious problem strikes into the wider pattern of popular piety, the 'religious' life, and late scholasticism.

That the word *Justitia* contained Luther's religious problem is important. It is even more momentous that within this word lay the tension between two mighty vocabularies, the Hellenic conception of Justice and the Biblical theme of the Righteousness of God. But for Luther *Justitia* was the problem, not to be softened by putting alongside it other ideas, such as the mercy (*misercordia*) or the goodness (*bonitas*) of God. Luther did not need to be told that all mediæval theologians had a doctrine of Grace and of Justification. The illumination came when, through this very conception 'Justice', there burst the saving intervention of a merciful God, displayed in Jesus Christ and freely bestowed on sinners. As Karl Holl has it, 'God does not send His Grace alongside His Righteousness, but He sends it through His Righteousness . . . this was more than a new exposition of Romans, 1. 17 . . . it was the fountain spring of a new doctrine of God.'[1]

[1] K. Holl, vol. iii, *Westen*, p. 188.

CHAPTER THREE

'IN EXITU ISRAEL'

'Then was Christian glad and lightsome and he said with a merry heart, "He hath given me rest by his sorrow and life by his death." Then he stood still awhile to look and wonder, for it was very surprising to him, that the sight of the Cross should thus ease him of his burden.'

WHEN LUTHER'S MONASTIC PRECEPTOR handed him a copy of the Bible, bound in red, he read it avidly, and we may suspect that, following the advice he later gave to Spalatin, he began at the beginning and read it through, not once or twice, but until his mind was drenched through and through with the Biblical material, and he could handle his Bible with a facility which was the marvel of his friends and the envy of his enemies.

It was natural that, for the matter of his first exegetical lectures, he should turn to the Psalms, for it would be difficult to exaggerate what the Psalter—'the Bible in miniature'—meant to him. The Psalms were the first considerable part of the Bible which he got by heart for use in cell and choir. Month by month the Divine offices moved through the Psalter with stately measure, touching the height and depth of every emotion, every mood and almost every human crisis. Now it was the poignant cry of Israel, ravished and discomforted, in exile among her foes; next the exultant joy that God's right arm had swept giant foes into oblivion; the long, backward glances down the corridor of the past, with their reminders against the folly and faithlessness of Israel, of the enduring faithfulness of God. The piteous complaint of the poor man, betrayed, defenceless, while the ungodly struts before him in insolence and pride; the shout of crowds at some high festival; the impatience of the saints, beset by temptation and anguish; music and dancing, the noisy clamour of the temple courts, the silent eloquence of the little hills, the valleys thick with corn, the great sea, the sun and the stars, the ancient offering of a contrite heart, and through them all the solemn testimony to the transitory glory of this world, against the abiding Word of God. No wonder Luther cried:

In short, would you see the Holy Christian Church painted with living colour and form, fastened together in one picture, take your Psalter, and you have a fine, clear, pure mirror which will show you what Christianity is.[1]

To it he returned again and again, and when he would console his Prince in sickness, or instruct a young man in the art of politics, or send a word of comfort to his own dying father, it was to expound the Psalms that he turned. 'The Psalter,' says Heinrich Bornkamm, 'linkea him with his own world by a thousand ties.'[2]

For to Luther and to his contemporaries, as we can hardly understand, the Psalter was a Christian book. It was not simply a manual illustrating the Religion of the Hebrews, from which, as from an embarrassingly narrow ethical and historical context, the scholar might withdraw some edifying platitudes. It was well that Luther came to break with the traditional fourfold method of scriptural exegesis he inherited, but there is reason to be glad he began with it. According to this, the Psalms could be interpreted, in the literal-prophetic sense, with reference to Christ; tropologically they related to the individual soul; allegorically to the Church; anagogically, to the eschatological end of all things.[3]

Used in a wooden way, the fourfold exegesis could excite the most fantastic, arid and unedifying speculations. But we may consider that, as applied to the Psalms and as first one and then another interpretation became paramount, it might yield rich meaning. To begin with, God's mighty acts in His Son, the groundwork of the historical revelation; then, the counterpart of these objectivities within the experience of each human soul; next, the reminder that the great biblical 'Thou' confronts the believer only within the Israel of God; finally, the knowledge that here all our solutions are broken, pertaining to man as stranger and pilgrim (*homo viator*) and beckoning beyond history

---

[1] *Preface to the Psalter* (1534).
[2] H. Bornkamm, *Luther und das Alte Testament*, Tübingen 1948, p. 8.
[3] E. Vogelsang, *Die Anfänge von Luthers Christologie nach der ersten Vorlesung*, Berlin 1929, pp. 19–21.

to the final consummation. As a framework of devotion, there is a good deal to be said for it, and it is a good deal richer than that of many modern Christians.

In an important essay, Vogelsang suggested the importance of this method for Luther. In the combination of the Christological and tropological interpretation of the 'Justice of God' in the Psalms, we find the clue to Luther's solution.

Thus he came to see the 'Justice of God' as a righteousness revealed in Jesus Christ and bestowed to man on the ground of faith. Without committing ourselves to the details of Vogelsang's further hypothesis that we can trace the exact point of impact of the discovery on Luther's lectures on the Psalms, viz. Ps. 70–71, we may believe that Luther did in fact make his discovery during the lectures on the Psalms, i.e. 1513–4.[1]

Perhaps too much has been read into Luther's so-called 'Tower Experience' (*Turmerlebnis*—from the room in the monastery at Wittenberg in which, according to the *Table Talk*, Luther came to a new understanding of Rom. 1. 17). We must not read into it any preconceived pattern on the lines of an evangelical 'conversion'. The attempt, on the other hand, to divorce Luther's religious problem from his theological research, seems still more unsatisfactory.[2]

Bornkamm's words are salutary: 'One thing is more and more clear from recent research: the inmost, most personal experience of Luther, and his scholarly, theological, above all exegetical discoveries cannot be separated . . . the secret lies . . . in the indissoluble unity of personal experience and theological and exegetical research.'[3] We might remember Luther's own words: 'I did not learn my theology all at once, but I had to search deeper for it, where my temptations took me.'[4]

The facts, then, may have been more humdrum than legend

---

[1] E. Vogelsang, *Anfänge*, p. 50. The difficult problems of the MSS. of these lectures have been sifted further by H. Wenndorf, *Der Durchbruch der neuen Erkenntnis Luthers im Lichte der handschriftlichen Uberlieferungen, Hist. Vierteljahrschrift*, 1932, pp. 124, 285. Wenndorf's strictures on Vogelsang's handling of the MSS. may be justified, but they do not shake the theological value of his essay. We shall not perhaps get much nearer than the general date 1513–14. See L. Pinomaa, *Der Existentielle Charakter der Theologie Luthers*, Helsinki 1940, pp. 130–7.

[2] As with U. Saarnivaara, *Luther's Path to Evangelical Faith*, Helsinki 1947.

[3] Boehmer, *Junge Luther* (ed. Bornkamm), pp. 362–3.

[4] TR 1.146.12.

suggests, less than that dramatic intervention in which, we con-
ceive, God is wont to deal with His servants the prophets. But it
is perhaps the way in which in His inscrutable wisdom He
addresses His theological professors. And we, who are considering Martin Luther, shall not have much to complain about in
the way of lack of excitement in what follows.

The discovery and publication of the material from which
Luther delivered his great courses of lectures in these years
(Psalms, 1513–4; Romans, 1515–6; Galatians, 1516–7; Hebrews,
1517–8) has been a great achievement of the last thirty years of
Luther studies, and it has revolutionized the conception of his
development. It is clear that, in all essentials, his theology was
in existence before the opening of the Church struggle in 1517.
The old polemical assertion that Luther lacked all originality is
untenable: no more than the paintings of Rembrandt, or the
music of Bach, can he be explained in terms of the past alone.
The Catholic Lortz says: 'Luther did not express many ideas to
which we can find no parallels from earlier theologians and
reformers. Nevertheless, Luther is new.'[1]

It has been said, with but slight exaggeration, that the whole
of the later Luther may be found in the lectures on the Psalms.[2]
Luther can still use the jargon of the schools, the distinctions of
Peter Lombard,[3] and Augustine is still a dominant theological
influence.[4]

He retains the doctrine of the *Syntheresis*—the inextinguishable
spark of the divine in man, which desires the good.[5] His
(and St. Paul's) great distinction between Law and Gospel
has yet to be developed.[6] But here, proof that it is no later
improvisation, are the outlines of his doctrine of the Church,
the theme of the Word of God, and the assertion that the Church
is intelligible to faith alone (*intelligibilis per fidem est ecclesia*). Here
is the demonstration that Luther no more thinks in terms of a
purely invisible Church than such modern Catholic writers as

---

[1] J. Lortz, *Reformation*, i, p. 147.
[2] K. Holl, *Luther*, p. 155.
[3] *ibid.* p. 156.
[4] A. Hamel, *Der Junge Luther und Augustin*, 2 vols. 1934–5.
[5] WA 3.535.36, 603.33; WA 4.255.24; Pinomaa, *Existentielle Charakter*,
p. 41; W. Loewenich, *Luthers Theologia Crucis*, Munich 1933, p. 56.
[6] Runestam, *Den kristliga Friheten hos Luther och Melanchthon*, Stockholm
1917, p. 44.

E. Mersch and H. de Lubac in their expositions of the doctrine of the Church as the Mystical Body.[1]

To turn from the lectures on the Psalms to those on Romans (1515–6) is to recall G. K. Chesterton's remark about H. G. Wells that you could almost hear him growing in the night, so plain is the growth in maturity, independence and coherence in a few months. There is still much of traditional orthodoxy, and of St. Augustine. But there is now a more radical diagnosis of the sin of man, the seat of which, under all disguises and idolatries, is his egoism, lifting itself in rebellion against God.[2] The repudiation of self (*accusatio sui*) is something a man cannot achieve without the inspiration of the Holy Spirit. Concupiscence is no longer for Luther the desire of the flesh, and inbred sin is more than a mere material, a tinder (*fomes peccati*); it is a restless egotism which is active and working even in our dreams.[3] Luther has discarded the psychological teaching of Aristotle of a *habitus* within the soul, and in its place is a new anthropology of the person, the whole man. It breaks with the Platonic and neo-Platonic division between soul and body and returns to the biblical division between 'flesh' and 'spirit', the conception of man as a sinner confronted in all his personal existence by the person of the living God.[4]

More clearly expressed than ever before, is the assertion that sinful man must find a righteousness which comes from without himself. 'For God wills to save us, not by a righteousness and wisdom from within [*per domesticam*] but from without [*per extraneam*] Not that which comes and is born from ourselves. But which comes from without into us. Not which rises from the earth, but that which comes down from heaven.'[5] 'For not because he is Just is a man reckoned to be so by God, but because he is reckoned to be just by God, therefore is he just.'

---

[1] WA 3.259.18, 139.19, 347.25 ff.; WA 4.183.17 ff., 189.17; Holl, *Luther*, pp. 288 ff.; H. Stomps, *Die Anthropologie Martin Luthers*, 1935.

[2] WA 56.356.4. 'And this agrees with Scripture, which describes man as turned in upon himself (*incurvatum in se*) so that not only in bodily but also in spiritual goods he turns to himself and seeks himself in all things.' 357.4, 357.11.

[3] See Holl, *Luther*, pp. 62 ff. and quotations.

[4] WA 56.343.16, 343.24. 'The whole man is "flesh" because the Spirit of God abide not in it.' Regin Prenter, *Spiritus Creator*, Copenhagen, 1946, 26.

[5] WA 56.158.10, 169.29, 172.3.

It is important to guard against misunderstanding at this point, for some of the wisest scholars have warned us against supposing we are here confronted with some abstract doctrine of the imputation of the merits of Christ like that of some forms of later Lutheran orthodoxy. The righteousness of God which is given to us is, as Prenter says, 'the living Christ in his own person'.[1] Faith is much more than an intellectual acceptance of new truth, 'that is why it would be impious just to doubt or think that a man is justified by faith, but it is necessary most certainly and firmly to believe it and to know it'.[2] Peter Lombard had suggested the identity of the Holy Spirit with the charity infused into the redeemed soul, but in Luther, as his discussion of Rom. 8. 26 shows, the Spirit is no longer a transcendant cause of salvation, but the living personal presence of God, at work, and interceding for us with groans that cannot be uttered.[3] There is a characteristically Lutheran stress on the gladness, willingness and spontaneity with which the Christian man obeys and loves the will of God.[4]

The unrighteous sinner may stand in the presence of God because his unrighteousness is lost 'in the infinite abyss of the righteousness of God'.[5] We cannot linger over the doctrine of sanctification in these lectures, or compare Karl Holl's discussion of it in the light of the formidable criticism his treatment has received from Scandinavian scholars in recent years.[6] Yet all are agreed that Luther's doctrine of justification in no wise contemplates a man remaining in his sins, with no prospect of ever leaving them. On the contrary, Luther returns again and again to the thought of movement and growth in the Christian life. 'Now they begin to be Christians whose life is not in rest, but in movement, from good to better, as a sick man moves from sickness to health.'[7] The threefold formula is important: 'Always a sinner, always a penitent, always right with God.'[8] Luther goes on to speak of the renewal of our minds day by day, and how the Spirit transforms our feelings and enables us to recognize the will of God.[9] Two illustrations recur in these

---

[1] Prenter, p. 67 ff.   [2] WA 56.39.18.   [3] WA 56.378.
[4] WA 56.366.14. 'To be led by the Spirit of God is freely, promptly, cheerfully to mortify the flesh, i.e. the old man.'
[5] WA 56.204.23.
[6] K. Holl, *Luther*, pp. 115–54; Prenter, *Spiritus Creator*, p. 60.
[7] WA 56.441.14.   [8] WA 56.442.17.   [9] WA 56.443.5, 446.5.

lectures. The first, taken from St. Augustine, the thought of Our Lord as the Good Samaritan who finds the sinner half dead, but who takes him in his care until he is cured. The second is the thought of God as some skilled master craftsman who can demonstrate his skill in three ways: first, when he corrects the mistakes and bad workmanship of his apprentices; second, when the excellence of his own work is shown by comparison of his work with theirs; but third, when he gives away his own skill, by teaching others the secrets of his own mystery, for the third, says Luther, shows his own 'benevolence' and *humanitas*, and so the 'just God is laudable in us, because he makes us like himself'.[1]

Whatever the date when Luther first began to be exercised about predestination, his notes on Rom. 8. 28 contain a poignant discussion of the problem, which anticipates his discussion in the *De Servo Arbitrio* (1525). Luther ends with a remarkable note. 'Here I must enter a warning, lest any whose minds have not been purged rush into these speculations and fall into an abyss of horror and despair: let him first purge the eyes of his heart in meditating the wounds of Jesus Christ. Nor would I talk about this, did not the order of the lectures and necessity compel me to do so. For this is the very strongest wine and the most perfect and solid food for the perfect. The most advanced theology! But I am as a child who needs milk, not food. Let those who are as I am, do likewise. The wounds of Jesus are safe enough for us.'[2]

It is a matter for discussion how far Staupitz helped Luther to come to this conclusion.[3] One other influence must be remarked. It has been suggested that Luther turned away from the traditional theology, and from the influence of St. Augustine, because at this time he came under the influence of the mystics.[4] We need to distinguish. The word 'mysticism' is often vaguely used to cover any kind of 'inward religion'. We ought, as Vogelsang suggests, to distinguish between the mysticism of the Victorines (and of the writings of Pseudo-Dionysius), which is to be discounted in Luther's case, and that of the Roman type of St.

[1] WA 56.221-2.
[2] WA 56.400.1.
[3] E. Wolf, *Staupitz und Luther*, pp. 169-222.
[4] Miegge, *Lutero*, p. 118 *n.*; H. Bornkamm, *Eckhart und Luther*, Stuttgart 1936, *Luther und Böhme*, 1925; J. M. Clark, *The Great German Mystics*, Oxford 1949.

Bernard which but slightly influenced him, and third, the mysticism of the *devotio moderna* in the German form in which it reached him in the writings of Tauler, and the little book known to us as the *Theologia Germanica*.

Luther became acquainted with Tauler's writings through his friend John Lang, in 1516, and in the next months spoke enthusiastically about his sermons and even more warmly about the little *Theologia Germanica*. Luther may have taken some of his terminology from these writings, but their value to him seems to be that they confirmed rather than inaugurated any doctrines, by their emphasis on 'inward religion' and on the wholly personal character of sin. We may compare the similarly real but peripheral influence of William Law upon the brothers Wesley at an early stage in their theological and religious development. But as Luther's own notes on Tauler show, he did not read him uncritically, and maintained a stern sense of the superiority of theology over mystical literature. Had he been under deep influence of the mystical writings, he could never, as he did at this time, have broken with the doctrine of the *Syntheresis*, the divine spark in man, a conception especially sympathetic to mystic thought.

In any case, Luther had come to a way through his temptations about predestination apart from them. The doctrine of resignation (*resignatio ad infernum*) in Luther is different from that of the mystics. Luther believed at this time that the soul might come to the point when it joyfully agreed to the will of God, even though that will might consign it to hell, and that such a resignation must, paradoxically, be a sign of grace and a hope of predestination! But it has been powerfully shown that Luther's thought is Christological: here is no abandonment (*Gelassenheit*) of the creature before the infinite God. Instead, Luther stresses the grim reality of the humiliation of Jesus Christ, in Gethsemane and on the Cross, and in the supreme cry of dereliction, and affirms that for us men and for our salvation Christ underwent the most hideous of temptations and trod the way of horror and despair.[1] Luther does not speak of the 'imitation of Christ' as conceived by the 'modern devotion' but of the conformity of the Christian with Christ, in death and resurrection and in living

[1] Vogelsang, *Angefochtene Christus*, pp. 81 ff.

faith. Anguish, tribulation, temptation (*Anfechtung*) are signs that the Christian really is in the hands of God, and is sharing the Cross of Christ. Salvation is appropriated not through abstract consideration of a doctrine of atonement, but through the recognition of the Living God whose strange work (*opus alienum*) it is to bring us through the Law and the Wrath to knowledge of divine and infinite mercy (*opus proprium*). Law is not for Luther an abstract principle of the universe. As Macbeth saw with horror Birnam Wood, which he had thought immovable, closing in on him since behind natural phenomena was personal direction, so for Luther the Law is the personal, saving activity of God himself, and the Wrath of God (which is no fiction) becomes the engine of salvation.

One of Luther's students (1518–22) has left us a vivid picture of him at his lectures:

He was a man of middle stature, with a voice which combined sharpness and softness: it was soft in tone, sharp in the enunciation of syllables, words and sentences. He spoke neither too quickly nor too slowly, but at an even pace, without hesitation, and very clearly, and in such fitting order that each part flowed naturally out of what went before. He did not expound each part in long labyrinths of words, but first the individual words, then the sentences, so that one could see how the content of the exposition arose, and flowed out of the text itself. For it all hung together in order, word, matter, natural and moral philosophy as the Dialectic of Philip [Melanchthon] teaches. For this was how he took it from a book of the essential matter, which he had himself prepared, so that he had his lecture material always ready to hand, conclusions, digressions, moral philosophy and also antitheses: and so his lectures never contained anything that was not pithy and relevant. And, to say something about the spirit of the man: if even the fiercest enemies of the Gospel had been among his hearers, they would have confessed from the force of what they heard, that they had witnessed, not a man, but a spirit, for he could not teach such amazing things from himself, but only from the influence of some good or evil spirit.[1]

Luther's other duties had grown formidably. Since 1511 he had been preaching in the monastery, and from 1514 in the parish church. In May, 1512, he became sub-prior and regent of the monastery school. In May, 1515, he was made

[1] *Der Junge Luther* (ed. Bornkamm), p. 367.

district overseer of eleven monasteries. He wrote wryly, complaining:

I do almost nothing but write letters all day long . . . I am conventual preacher, reader at meals, sought for to preach daily in the parish church, am regent of studies, district Vicar (i.e. eleven times Prior), inspect the fish ponds at Leitzkau, act in the Herzberg affair at Torgau, lecture on St. Paul, revising my Psalms, . . . I seldom have time to go through my canonical hours properly, or to celebrate, to say nothing of my own temptations from the world, the flesh and the devil. You see what a lazy fellow I am.[1]

Meanwhile, Luther's teaching had excited more and more bitter opposition from the Gabrielists at Erfurt, and there was rising tension at Wittenberg itself. It came to a head at a public disputation on September 25th, 1516, when Luther, for this special occasion, presided while his pupil Bartholomew Bernhardi defended a series of theses about grace and the human will, which directly attacked the Nominalist teaching.[2] But the sensation of the day came when Luther himself caused an uproar among his own colleagues by denying the authenticity of Augustine's *True and False Penitence*,[3] a writing often quoted in the *Sentences of Peter Lombard* (Bk. IV, Dist. 14–17) and which Luther asserted had been used to torture the consciences of simple folk. Andreas Karlstadt fumed, and went off to Leipzig as soon as he could to get the book. He returned, not only converted to Luther's opinion, but more enthusiastically Lutheran than Luther. The disputation had certainly cleared the air.

With the autumn mists, the plague came to Wittenberg, but Luther wrote to Lang:

Where should I fly? The world won't come to an end when brother Martin does [he was to write the same sentiment to his wife in almost the last letter of his life]. I shall send the brothers away, if the plague gets worse. I am stationed here and may not run away because of my vow of obedience, until the same authority which bids me stay, commands me to depart. Not that I do not fear the plague (I am not the Apostle Paul, but only a lecturer on him) but I hope the Lord will deliver me from my fear.[4]

[1] WA Br.1 (October 26th, 1516), p. 72.
[2] WA 1.145.1 ff.
[3] WA Br.1 (October, 1516) p. 65, 1.25.
[4] WA Br.1.73.34.

He was now quite clear in his mind about the Nominalists. 'I am not going to dispute whether Gabriel said this, or Raphael that, or Michael the other thing. I know what Gabriel says, and he says everything well—except when he talks about grace, charity, hope, faith, the virtues, about which he Pelagianizes as much as his Scotus.'[1] In February, 1517, he felt constrained to carry the war into the opposite camp, and he sent a series of propositions against Aristotelian theology to Trutvetter, via Lang, in which he poured out his deep indignation. 'The greatest part of my cross is to see brothers, with brilliant gifts, born for good studies, and yet compelled to spend their life and waste their achievement in these follies.'[2]

But in Wittenberg, the battle had been won. In May, he could write:

Our theology and St. Augustine are going ahead, and reign in our University, and it is God's work. Aristotle is gradually going down, perhaps into eternal ruin. It is wonderful how the lectures on the *Sentences* are out of favour. Nobody can hope for an audience unless he professes this theology, i.e. the Bible or St. Augustine, or some doctor of real authority in the Church.[3]

He could not let matters rest there, without a sense of responsibility for the other teaching centres of his order, and in the autumn he decided on a bold step. At the promotion of Franz Gunther to the degree of Bachelor, he put forward a series of ninety-seven Theses: they were a careful and direct attack on the whole Nominalist position, Gabriel Biel, William of Occam, Peter D'Ailly, with a few spare shots at Scotus and 'many other doctors'.[4] It seems probable that Luther had them printed and sent to Erfurt and to Nuremberg. He wanted them publicly debated, and offered to go to Erfurt himself to defend his propositions in the university or in the monastery. His letter to Lang shows how anxiously he awaited the outcome, and with what long deliberation he had taken this step. 'They need not think I have done this thing in a corner, if indeed our University is so mean that it seems like a corner.'[5] It may have been the most carefully planned act of public defiance of Luther's career, and it seems completely to have misfired. Here, surely, might have been the opening broadside of a great controversy to shake

---

[1] WA Br.1.66.3.   [2] WA Br.1.88.24.   [3] WA Br.1.99.8.
[4] WA 1.224 ff.   [5] WA Br.1.103.14.

Germany in a way second only to the Reuchlin affair. But nothing happened, and it seemed that Luther was not destined to live in history as a reformer of university studies. Not for the first, or the last, time did Luther find his best plans came to nothing, while immense and unintended consequences came when least expected.

By the autumn of 1517 Luther had come a long way. We misunderstand entirely if we think of him as a restless innovator, or, in Gerhard Ritter's fine phrase, as a kind of academic bully. When Holl calls Luther's religion the religion of conscience, it is not due to Holl's Kantianism, or Luther's subjectivism. But Luther's fight was within his conscience, and it was in the City of Mansoul he learned the art of the warfare he would one day carry to the gates of Gath, and into the streets of Askelon. His anger against the Nominalist teaching, and the Aristotelian domination of the schools, was that they were leading souls astray, fobbing men off with a false security, which failed them, as Luther had seen again and again, when they stood terrified by the fact of death. But conscience for Luther meant facing the Wrath of God, rather than preoccupation with his own emotions, and so led directly to the great saving objectivities of his *Theology of the Cross*.

He had learned that the Christian warfare is the fight of faith, faith which may run counter to all human thoughts, feelings and experiences, since it is by faith that our lives are hid with Christ in God. There is no finer or more illuminating saying of Luther's in these years than that uttered during his lectures on the Epistle to the Hebrews:

It is a great matter, to be a Christian man, and to have a hidden life, hidden away, not in some place like a hermit, nor in his own heart, though that is an unsearchable depth, but in the invisible God himself, and to live thus in the world, but to feed on that which is never seen, except by way of the Word and only through the medium of hearing.[1]

[1] *Hebrews* (ed. Hirsch), Ruckert, Berlin 1929, p. 235.

CHAPTER FOUR

THE HUBBUB

*'One chanced mockingly, beholding the carriage of the men, to
say unto them, "What will you buy?" But they, looking
gravely upon them, said, "We buy the Truth." At that there
was occasion taken to despise the men the more, some taunting,
some speaking reproachfully, and some calling on others to
smite them. At last things came to a hubbub, insomuch that
all order was confounded.'*

THE WRATH OF GOD, as a clue to the interpretation of history,
is out of fashion, relegated among those categories characterized
by the Master of Trinity as 'pietistic flapdoodle'. The moralizing
of Carlyle or Froude has given place to the doctrinaire anti-
nomianism of the modern historian who listens to the past as a
psychiatrist to a patient, determined at all costs never at any
point in the story to be shocked. Yet what men have believed
about history is itself part of the story. When Michelangelo
scrawled over the Pope's private chapel the vision of Judgment,
and of a Christ risen in wrath, his arm forked like the lightning,
a Christ, as J. A. Symonds has it, who is 'what the sins of Italy
and the Church have made him', he tells us something about
the sixteenth century which is important for our understanding
of that age. And something apart from which we cannot understand Martin Luther.

The Church is the New Israel, the People of God. The history
of the Hebrew people tells us that when the heirs of the divine
promises rebel, deny, forsake their pastoral and evangelical
vocation, there follows, in real history, inexorable and grim
disaster. 'For every false word or unrighteousness, for cruelty
and oppression, for lust or vanity, the price has to be paid at
last: not always by the chief offenders, but paid by somebody—
Doomsday comes at last.' But Froude's moralizing is, as he
acknowledged, only an echo of the Book of Amos.

What, then, is the application to Church history? What are the inexorable consequences of the sins of the New Israel? What is the historical entail of the misdeeds, not of Political or Economic Man, but of Ecclesiastical Man, who has done so much to bedevil European history, and who reached his apogee in the late Middle Ages? What happens when the successors of the Apostles betray, deny, forsake their evangelical vocation? And what shall be done in the end thereof? It is a question which the Church has never willingly faced, but always deferred until Doomsday, for great masses of men have rarely been moved to drastic reform save under the impulse of grave disaster. But Doomsday has come, when the Church has had to face in history itself the consequences of its unassoiled sins. The Reformation is—ordeal by History. We shall see how when the Pope tried to deal with Martin Luther, the history of a thousand years intervened, with its political intrigue, juridical chicanery, moral laxity, and in the Curia itself a levity and indifference on the part of many high ecclesiastics, in sad contrast to the deep earnestness of the man they arraigned.

M. Gilson made a penetrating criticism of the Reformers when he accused them, in philosophy and theology, of failure to appreciate the importance of secondary causes. There is a worse fault, to have allowed the prime vocation, the pastoral care, to sink to the bottom of an agenda which became more and more elaborate as the whole machinery of the Church became entangled in social, political, juridical pressures. These things are freely granted by Catholic historians. But we must ask what could be the result in history of the fact that almost all the defects of the late mediæval Church touched this supreme issue. 'The hungry sheep look up and are not fed.' When the Shepherds of Israel evoked the prophetic indictment of Ezekiel, the Wrath of God was seen to be at work in inexorable historical tragedy, involving innocent and guilty. That the Shepherds of the New Israel should bring doom upon their age is a judgment which, no doubt, begs a number of important questions, though in the end the conception of the Wrath of God as an ingredient of history gives more scope for righteousness and mercy than the current popular theme of history as the dialectic of the wrath of man.

Protestants have often overdarkened the shadows. We need

not fear to acknowledge that, as the Conciliar movement had shown, the Church could produce men of learning, piety, genius, at least in as high a proportion as the modern ecumenical movement. The fifteenth century could produce a Savonarola, Geiler of Keysersberg, Thomas à Kempis, Nicholas of Cusa, Gabriel Biel. Indeed, when we consider the early sixteenth century, we may wonder if the worst had not already passed. Were these men sinners above all others? Here some suggestive words of Kingsley may be remembered: 'It is not the worst, but often the best specimens of a class or of a system who are swallowed up by the moral earthquake, which has been accumulating its forces, perhaps for centuries . . . so far from being sinners above all around them, they are often better people than those around them. It is as if they were punished, not for being who they were, but for being what they were.'[1]

It is true that a culture was dying, and that much of the life of the Church was entangled with it. If there are revivals of religion, there are revivals also of superstition, though these are less often chronicled, and the paintings of Jerome Bosch remind us of the diablerie, the revival of Gnostic cults, of astrology, the dark background of a 'failure of nerve' against which the growth of witchcraft and witch hunting have to be observed. But what was dying, like the Holy Roman Empire, and what had the secret of inner renewal, like the Papacy, was not easy to discern. A strange world was being born, its birth pangs a series of political and social tensions which baffled statesmen to comprehend, let alone resolve, while for one new world across the Atlantic to attract the bodies of men, a dozen new horizons of the mind were opening, offering the Church that challenge to baptize a culture which in the first, the fifth, the ninth centuries she had marvellously accepted, but which now, sick, enfeebled and in sin, she was unable to comprehend.

Nine out of ten men did not ponder such high themes. They worked hard, produced children and watched too many of them die, they drank beer and grumbled, and reckoned with the Church when and where it touched their own souls, in their prayers and in their pockets; and in one matter, the Indulgence affair, in a combination of both.

Over the whole doctrine of the Church, of the papal authority,

[1] C. Kingsley, 'The Judgments of God', *Westminster Sermons*, p. 237.

the doctrine of merit, the doctrine of indulgences, there reigned an uncertainty and vagueness which Lortz regards as a prime cause of the Reformation, and not least of the hesitant attitude of the orthodox with regard to Luther's teachings. The Indulgence was primarily the commutation of the act of satisfaction which was one of the three parts of the Sacrament of Penance (contrition; confession; satisfaction). In 1300 Boniface VIII issued a Jubilee Indulgence to all who visited the tombs of the Apostles on fifteen successive days: originally limited to one-hundred-year intervals, the Jubilees became more and more frequent as papal financial difficulties deepened. The practice found theoretical justification in the doctrine of the Treasure of Merits of Christ and the Saints, expounded by Alexander of Hales (*Summa*, IV, qu. 83) and confirmed in the Bull *Unigenitus* of Clement VI, 1343, which includes the statement that Christ 'acquired a treasure for the Church militant'. In 1476 Pope Sixtus IV extended the scope of an Indulgence to the souls in purgatory. By the beginning of the sixteenth century, Indulgences had become a holy business (*sacrum negotium*) so complex as to demand the superintendence of the Banking House of Fugger.

In 1513 the young Hohenzollern Prince Albert of Brandenburg (aged twenty-three) became Archbishop of Magdeburg and administrator of the diocese of Halberstadt. In 1514 there fell to him a more glittering prize, the Archbishopric of Mainz and the Primacy of Germany. Enormous fees were due to the Pope for this accumulation of benefices, and Albert was soon heavily in debt to the accommodating but watchful Fuggers. It was finally decided that when the Indulgence should be promulgated on behalf of rebuilding St. Peter's, Rome, half the proceeds should, by private agreement, go to Albert and the Fuggers. To this indulgence were attached four privileges: 'The first, the plenary remission of all sins; the second, a confessional letter allowing the penitent to choose his confessor; the third is the participation in the merits of the saints; the fourth is for the souls in purgatory.' Albert's own instructions to his sub-commissary are carefully worded to include the phrase *corde contritus et ore confessus*, i.e. they presuppose contrition and confession. But the pardoners went less discreetly to work. The literature of ecclesiastical rebuilding schemes rarely attains the higher levels of edification, but the sermons of John Tetzel (1470–1519), the Dominican charged to dispose of Indulgences in Saxony and Brandenburg, touched new depths.

The indulgence procession moved from town to town with the devout furore of a modern ecclesiastical exhibition. 'The Bull was borne on a satin, or gold-embroidered cushion, and all the priests and monks, the town council, schoolmaster, scholars, men, women, maidens and children went out to meet him with banners and tapers, with songs and processions. Then all the bells were rung, all the organs played . . . a red Cross was erected in the midst of the church, and the Pope's banner displayed.'[1]

Financial embarrassment was not confined to the Pope, or to Albert of Mainz. Shortage of coin led most German rulers to be chary of letting currency leave their territories. Frederick the Wise had little love for the new Archbishop, and the Indulgence was prohibited in Electoral Saxony. This did not greatly inconvenience the Wittenbergers, who could go off to Zerbst and Juterbogk, a few miles off, to return with extravagant stories about the sermons they had heard, and with pardons which some of them flourished in the presence of Luther.

For Luther it was no new concern, for he had already spoken publicly on the subject. True, it was a delicate matter to raise in Wittenberg, for within the Castle Church reposed Frederick the Wise's rapidly expanding collection of relics. From 5005 in 1509, they had grown in 1518 to 17,443 particles (including 204 portions and one whole corpse of the Holy Innocents!) and to them was now attached an indulgence of 127,799 years and 116 days.[2] On the other hand, for Luther to protest against Albert of Mainz was to invite the public suspicion that he was but the tool of the jealous interests of the House of Wettin. But the Indulgence caused a good deal of comment, and in public and in private Luther had been asked for his advice.

Once again, he sat down and wrote a series of Theses. He wrote fluently, for he had a gift for this kind of pithy, aphoristic paradox, and if there were some points on which he was un-

[1] B. J. Kidd, *Documents of the Continental Reformation*, Oxford 1911, v, pp. 6, 8, 9; H. Boehmer, *Road to Reformation*, pp. 167 ff.; Mackinnon, ii, pp. 290–305; H. E. Jacobs, *Martin Luther*, New York 1898, pp. 59 ff.; Preserved Smith, *Life and Letters of M. Luther*, p. 36.

[2] Scheel, *Luther*, ii, pp. 333–4.

certain, and which went beyond his own definite conviction, these were, after all, Latin theses for disputations which traditionally had a good deal of licence.

He took them over, it seems, to his printer, John Grunenberg, and asked him to run off a few copies for his own private use. One he despatched with a covering letter to Albert of Mainz, and the other to his ordinary, the Bishop of Brandenburg. But he consulted nobody, and let nobody at the court know of his intentions. About midday, on the Eve of All Saints', he strolled with Agricola the length of the little town, along the streets which to-morrow would be thronged with the faithful. He mounted the steps of the Schlosskirche and affixed his placard, as he had a right to do, and in the normal way: 'In the desire and with the purpose of elucidating the truth, a disputation will be held . . .'; at first sight no more exciting than most notices on most university boards. He turned away and went home, and no doubt ate a hearty meal. Yet this was far from casual: 'I had first prostrated myself in prayer that God would be with me.'[1] There was the ominous fact that nobody attended the disputation.

It might seem as though the operative text of the Reformation was not 'The just shall live by faith', but 'Concerning the collection'. Yet, although the ninety-five Theses on the 'Power and efficacy of Indulgences' do not mention 'Faith' or 'Justification', to read them is to be reminded again and again of the road along which Luther's thought had moved.[2] The last two Theses, and the last three words of all are revealing: 'Christians should be exhorted that they study to follow Christ, their head, through the pains of death and hell [94] and let them rather hope to enter heaven through much tribulation than to confide in the security of peace' [*Per securitatem pacis confidant*]. For it was this same 'security' which Luther had again and again attacked, the terrible false security which could delude simple men into believing that the Wrath of God could be appeased by a money payment to God's commissaries, what a modern Lutheran martyr (Dietrich Bonhoeffer) has called the doctrine of 'cheap grace' against the doctrine of 'costly grace'. In Luther's great

[1] TR 5.658.1.
[2] Wace and Bucheim, *Luther's Primary Works*, pp. 414 ff.; *Works of Martin Luther* (A. J. Holman, Philadelphia), vol. i, 13 ff.; *M. Luther's 95 Theses* (Kleine Texte 142); H. Bornkamm, *Luther's Geistige Welt*, Luneburg 1947, pp. 39 ff.

conviction (62) 'the true treasure of the Church is the Holy Gospel of the Glory and the Grace of God'. Or turn to the first Thesis: 'When Our Lord and Master Jesus Christ said *Poenitentiam Agite* . . . he wished the entire life of believers to be one of penitence . . .' with the reminiscence of his own discovery of the inwardness of repentance through the offices of Staupitz, the echo of his own aphorism in his 'Romans'—'*semper peccator, semper PENITENS, semper Justus.*'

For the rest, they are no revolutionary manifesto. The authority of the Pope is affirmed. The existence of Purgatory is taken for granted. Thesis 71 says: 'Let him who speaks against the truth of apostolic pardons be accursed and anathema.' It is true that there is an edge to these admissions, and a sharp comparison with the true Christian priorities, the duty to preach the Word of God, and to perform works of charitable service.

We hear much nowadays of the importance of 'technics' in society. Rarely has one invention had more decisive influence than that of printing on the Reformation. Luther's Theses were printed and translated into German, reprinted and posting through Germany in a fortnight, and circulating everywhere within a few weeks. In March, 1518, Luther was annoyed to get printed and translated copies of his Theses from his Nuremberg friend, Cristopher Scheuerl.: 'For I have certain doubts about them myself, and should have spoken differently and more distinctly, had I known what was going to happen.'[1] He had invited a public disputation, and nobody had come to dispute. Now, by a stroke of magic, he found himself addressing the world. All he could do was write a long and careful exposition of his Theses, and send these 'Resolutions' to the Bishop of Brandenburg. To him he explained his original intention, to provoke a learned and public discussion, and how his plans had gone astray, from their publication in the vulgar tongue. He persisted, however, in his plea for full discussion. But he made plain he had not intended to act impertinently. 'I submit all things to the judgment of holy Church,' and he begged the Bishop to take pen in hand and strike through anything amiss.[2] We are not to suppose that Luther was dissembling. At the end of his life he could affirm (1545): 'When I took up this matter

[1] WA Br.1.152.13.   [2] WA Br.1.139.

against Indulgences, I was so full and drunken, yea, so besotted in papal doctrines, that out of my great zeal I would have been ready to murder—at least I would have been glad to see and help that murder should be done—on all who would not be obedient and subject to the Pope, even to his smallest word.'[1] Luther also published in German some notes of a sermon on the subject of Indulgences, at the end of which the first glow of his future polemical power may be discerned.

Authority had taken action. Albert of Mainz had forwarded the documents to Rome, with the request that Luther be inhibited. In February, 1518, orders to this effect were handed to Gabriel della Volta, pro-magistrate of the Augustinian Order, and the command was transmitted to Staupitz.

The serious danger came from the Dominicans. At their Saxon Chapter in January, 1518, Wimpina and Tetzel propounded a series of counter-Theses, and formally charged Luther at Rome on suspicion of heresy. The German Dominicans were soon boasting that Luther would be burned, and there must have been many at the time who saw in the controversy just one more squabble among the always quarrelling religious. Tetzel sent eight hundred copies of his Theses to Wittenberg, where the adventurous colporteur was roughly manhandled by the students who made a bonfire of the documents, winning a reprimand from the authorities, since the tumult could hardly have helped Luther at this delicate juncture. Luther's greatest ally was his friend and admirer Spalatin (1484–1548), librarian, secretary and chaplain to the Elector Frederick, and throughout these critical months it would be hard to exaggerate the debt he owed him. Alarmed though Luther's fellow Augustinians might be (they begged him not to bring the Order into discredit),[2] they had no intention of throwing him to the Dominicans. So Luther set out in April, 1518, for the Chapter at Heidelberg, despite alarming rumours, and provided with letters of credence of such high testimony that one official exclaimed, 'By God, that's a fine passport they've given you!'[3]

Luther did the long journey on foot, and not all the soft beauties of the Neckar in spring could assuage his physical

[1] WML 1.10.   [2] WA 31.i.111.34, 40.iii.620.32.   [3] WA Br.1.173.21.

exhaustion. When the Chapter opened, far from being in disgrace, the occasion became an unexpected and personal
triumph. He was relieved of the post of District Vicar, which
was given to his friend Lang, but this was a wise tactical move,
and it must in the circumstances have been a welcome relief.
Luther himself presided at a full-dress theological disputation
where the Indulgences were forgotten, and once more the battle
raged around the Aristotelian Nominalism and the new antidote proffered by Wittenberg. Luther's Heidelberg Theses rank
high among his theological writings, and in recent years Walther
von Loewenich has made them the starting point for an
illuminating exposition of Luther's *Theology of the Cross*.[1] Luther
sharply distinguishes between the 'Theology of the Cross'—
'thus the true theology is in Christ crucified, and there is the
true knowledge of God'—and the 'Theology of Glory', a
theology of speculation on the attributes of deity which is
ignorant that 'God is not found save in sufferings and in the
Cross'.[2]

It may be that Luther has not yet emerged from his
Augustinian tendency to put 'humility' in the place of 'faith',
but here, clearly established, is his now normative division
between the ministry of the Law and of the Gospel, the
first as God's Strange Work (*opus alienum*), and the second,
God's own work (*opus proprium*) by which he makes sinners
righteous.[3]

The debate was lively and there was some opposition, but
when the junior Heidelberg divine shouted angrily, 'If the
peasants heard that, they would stone you!' his voice was
drowned in general laughter.[4] But it was among the younger
men that Luther made his conquests that day. One of them, the
young Alsatian Dominican, Martin Bucer, was overwhelmed,
and wrote home in high glee because he managed to have lunch
with Staupitz and Luther:

Their wiles were not able to move him an inch ... his sweetness in
answering is remarkable [Bucer was not always to find it so remarkable in respect of himself!], his patience in listening is incomparable,
in his explanations you would recognize the acumen of Paul, not

[1] W. von Loewenich, *Luther's Theologia Crucis*, Munich 1933.
[2] WA 1.362.   [3] WA Br.1.173.   [4] WA 1.361.

Scotus: his answers, so brief, so wise and drawn from the Scriptures, easily made all hearers his admirers.[1]

Two other notable converts among the young men were John Brenz and Theodore Billicanus. The Reformation, like every other movement, cut through the generations, and the older men were not much impressed.

Luther got a lift back, and travelled part of the way with his old teacher, Usingen. As the wagon jolted and rumbled along, Luther poured out his soul with eager fire, but the time and the place were not propitious for a seminar, and he left the old man glum and silent, and a little dazed. To be cooped up with Martin Luther at close quarters, in this exuberant stage of his career, was apt to be a wearing experience. On his way through Erfurt, Luther tried to see his other old teacher, Trutvetter, but the old man was too ill to receive him, though Luther sent him an affectionate note disclaiming any intention of making a personal attack on Trutvetter 'to whom I owe everything', but explaining his own position: 'I am of the plain conviction that it is impossible to reform the Church, unless the Canon Laws, the decretals, the scholastic theology, philosophy, logic as they now are, are uprooted from the foundations, and other studies put in their place. To you I may not seem much of a logician, and perhaps I am not: but I do know this, that I fear nobody's logic in defending this thesis.'[2]

In May, Luther sent a copy of his *Resolutions*, with a letter of humble appeal, to Pope Leo X. The contrast between Luther's first draft and the fair copy reminds us that it was probably overseen by Spalatin and Staupitz, the first of many curious examples of what happened when Luther tried to temper his own forthright vehemence to the diplomacy of more tactful friends. In the same month, the Dominican Chapter met in Rome, and Tetzel was awarded a doctorate (a year later, discredited and disgraced, he was to die in Leipzig). Matters now took a more serious turn in Luther's case. In March (14th) he had preached a fiery sermon about the notorious abuse of the power of excommunication for trivial offences. Two Dominicans, who probably attended for the purpose, extracted articles from their notes, exaggerated them, and despatched them with some

[1] P. Smith, *Luther's Correspondence*, Philadelphia 1915, p. 82.
[2] WA Br.1.169–70.

even more dubious gossip to Rome, but not before they had enlisted the interest of the Emperor, through the Cardinal Cajetan. On the ground of this spurious information, Luther was declared to be a notorious heretic, and the formal sixty days' citation to Rome interrupted by a new order to Cajetan to arrest Luther, to demand that the Elector surrender him, and to order the Augustinian authorities in Germany to carry out the arrest.

CHAPTER FIVE

GREAT ARGUMENT

'The Judge directed his speech to the prisoner at the bar, saying, "Thou runagate, heretic, and traitor, hast thou heard what these honest gentlemen have witnessed against thee?"
FAITHFUL: *May I speak a few words in my own defence?*
JUDGE: *Sirrah! Sirrah! Thou deservest to live no longer, but to be slain immediately, yet that all men may see our gentleness towards thee, let us hear what thou, vile runagate, hast to say.'*

THE LUTHER MEMORIAL in the City of Worms is what we might expect of a near contemporary of the Albert Memorial in London. Even the egregious Baedeker who, like charity in St. Paul, is always eager to believe the best, can only say about it that it looks well enough in the early morning (*Morgenbeleuchtung günstig*). In the centre, an enormous Luther (3.2 metres high) gazes skyward with fixed intensity (heroic faith!), cuddling an enormous Bible. And there, among a number of lesser worthies, stands the figure (2.8 metres high) of the Elector Frederick the Wise.

The Elector Frederick earned his place on the memorial. He could have had little sympathy with Luther's theological protest against Indulgences. But he had a lively concern for his University and respect for all he had heard of Martin Luther. He had enough patriotism, not least where the Italians were concerned, to be unwilling to sacrifice Luther as a gambit to the cruel mercies of the Curia. But it is well to remember that at almost any time, had he so willed, the Elector could have ended the career of Martin Luther, and that it was due to him that Wittenberg remained for Luther the strangely calm centre of the cyclonic storm which raged all around.

When one considers the short shrift given to the Cambridge Reformers in England in the next two decades, one can only marvel at the fatal delays, hesitations, and patience of the

59

Roman authorities, and seek the reason in the realm of politics. For, just now, the Pope needed Frederick's goodwill. The arrangements for the succession in the Empire were under consideration, and the Pope was most unwilling that the House of Habsburg should find further aggrandizement. An order was sent to Cajetan that he should interview Luther at Augsburg, and that though there could be no question of argument with Luther, all possible deference must be shown towards the Elector. The Pope also intended the signal compliment of the Golden Rose.

Luther was now in deadly danger, uncertain from day to day that he might not be the price of some diplomatic deal in high places. Staupitz, whose heart made up in warmth what it lacked in stoutness, could only write gloomy encouragement— 'You have only the Cross to expect. Leave Wittenberg while there is still time, and come to me, so that we might live and die together.' Luther went to Weimar, however, to receive his expenses and letters of recommendation through Spalatin (he never spoke more than a dozen words to the Elector in his life). At length he arrived in Augsburg, *pauper et pedester*, afraid and sick at heart. Now, one individual, he must meet the angry engine of the mightiest institution in the world, the accumulated majesty of centuries, speaking with the authority of God himself. His fears were not lessened when the two Saxon councillors in the city warned him, in view of rumours, not to go near the Cardinal without a safe conduct.

Even a modern schoolboy knows of Luther's defiance at Worms, though the traditional utterance may be apocryphal. But in 1521 it was plain that half Germany was at Luther's side. If we look for a moment and a saying to admire, then we must turn to this moment in Augsburg, with Luther alone indeed (his friend had gone off to look for Staupitz) when the Italian diplomat Urban de Serralonga visited him, putting into words Luther's own secret doubts and fears, and ending with the capital taunt, 'Do you really think the Elector is going to war on your account?' Luther: 'By no means.' Urban: 'And where will you go then?' Luther: '*Sub Coelo*' (Under heaven). We do Luther less than justice if we underrate the earnestness of his words, of his naïve confidence that a man might go out, like Abraham, knowing not whither, and find his God a sufficient guard against a world in arms.

Perhaps because he had faced his own fears openly, the interview cheered him. Then came the four momentous interviews with Cajetan himself, a theologian of parts. If Luther had been so simple as to suppose authority would bandy words with him, he was soon speedily disillusioned. The Cardinal told him he was to do three things: repent and revoke his errors, promise not to teach them again, and refrain from all future mischievous activities. The veneer of etiquette soon wore thin and the Cardinal found, willy-nilly, that he was entangled in a wrangle about the meaning of the word 'Treasure' in the Bull *Unigenitus*. The Bull, Cajetan condescended to explain, means that 'Christ acquired a treasure', and this treasure consists of the merits of Christ and His saints. He was flabbergasted when Luther denied this. In fact, whatever the Bull might imply, it did not explicitly state the connection between the 'treasure' and the merits of Christ and the saints. For Luther this was more than a verbal quibble, for it was this very ambiguity which underlay his Theses 56–62, which culminated in the affirmation: 'The real treasure of the Church is the Holy Gospel of the Glory and the Grace of God' (Cajetan's haste, in the following days, to get some clear confirmation of his own exposition from Rome, is a sign that Luther had found a real loophole). Other interviews were not more successful, and the Cardinal haughtily denied 'bandying' words with Luther. When, on October 14th, Luther produced a written statement, Cajetan spoke of it so contemptuously that Luther's pent-up emotions burst out: voices were raised on both sides, and the Cardinal cut short the interview, telling Luther not to come near him again unless he were ready to recant. He saw Staupitz and Link privately, however, with a view to using their influence upon the obstinate monk. Affairs reached an impasse which only action could break. On October 16th Staupitz and Link judged matters to be so dangerous as to demand their own hasty withdrawal from the city. Luther wrote a formal appeal to the Pope and a long letter to Cajetan. As hours and days slipped away in ominous silence, Luther's friends became alarmed, and finally, in view of a persistent rumour that he was to be seized and sent in chains to Rome, they panicked. Luther was suddenly bundled out through a postern gate, ill clad and ill mounted, and he rode until forced to stop from exhaustion. A letter from Spalatin a few days later told him he had got away just in time.[1]

The Cardinal was furious at the defection, and wrote a stern letter to the Elector complaining of Luther's insolence. He had given Luther a hearing, and Luther had made plain the depth of his errors, 'part of them contrary to the teaching of the Apostolic See, and part of them damnable errors—and believe me, Your Grace, I know what I am talking about'. The letter ended with a contemptuous reference to Luther (*fraterculus*). Frederick passed it to Luther, who wrote a long and careful reply (his life might depend on it). He charged Cajetan with breaking his promises to the Elector, since all along there had been no discussion such as he had demanded, and since judgment had been passed on him before he had been heard. But Luther ended, 'I am willing to leave your territory and go wherever the merciful God would have me go.'

It seemed that go Luther must, though the Elector did not relish losing his pet theological professor to the King of France. At the end of November Luther said farewell to the Wittenbergers. On December 1st he gave a farewell supper, in the course of which two letters dramatically arrived, the first, expressing through Spalatin the Elector's surprise that Luther was not already gone, the second saying that if he had not departed he was to remain, in view of new and urgent matters which must be discussed. It seems probable that the change of plan was due to the appearance of the Papal emissary, Charles von Miltitz. On December 18th the Elector made up his mind. He would not send Luther to Rome, or into exile, unless he were first duly heard and properly convicted.

In the interval, happier events had occurred. The Elector was concerned that humanist studies at Wittenberg should not lag behind those at other universities, and had been prevailed upon to instal a Professor of Greek (to be followed by a Professor of Hebrew). In Germany there were more impecunious humanist scholars than pensions and professorial stipends, so that there was the usual polite jostling and touting. It looked as though the prize must go to the tedious Mosellanus from Leipzig, when it was suddenly announced that the post would be

---

[1] Mackinnon, ii, pp. 72–92; Boehmer, *Road to Reformation*, pp. 230, 244; Bainton, *Church History* (September, 1947), p. 174.

filled by a young prodigy, a beardless boy, nephew of the great Hebraist Reuchlin, Philip Melanchthon (1497–1560). He was small, thin, with an enormous brow, looking so absurdly youthful that one would have liked to hear Luther's comment when the new professor (aged twenty-one) announced as the subject of his Inaugural 'On the Reform of Adolescent Studies'! But the address itself, a mature and scholarly programme of humanist reform, was swift to win hushed respect and, at the end, wondering applause. Soon the new professor was lecturing to crowded audiences of several hundreds of students, where dons and undergraduates jogged one another's elbows in a zest for note taking. Luther wrote to his friends with huge glee, and with characteristic generosity declared that this young colleague surpassed himself, not only in polite letters, but in theological exposition. It was the beginning of an historic friendship. Luther's was the stronger character, but in some measure each supplied the defects of the other, while both owed more than they knew to this enduring bond which at times became sadly strained, but which never broke.

On January 12th, 1519, the old Emperor Maximilian died. 'Kaiser Max' as warrior, hunter and mountaineer, had greatly appealed to German sentiment, but his mixture of family and imperial ambition had fatally weakened his achievement, and he had opposed the constitutional reforms within Germany proposed by the 'Peace and Order' movement of Archbishop Berthold of Mainz (1484–1504)[1]. His nephew Charles came from the Netherlands, and brought a fateful association with Spain: he would represent such an accumulation of Imperial power as had never been wielded since the days of the Emperor Charles the Great. The Pope exerted full pressure to prevent the Empire passing to the formidably encircling sovereignty of Charles, and he was willing rather to favour the claims of Francis I of France or even of the Elector Frederick. The result was that in the matter of Luther the delaying tactics of the Saxon court found full scope. On March 29th the Pope wrote Luther a note gentler in tone than any previous communication. In June the word was passed to Frederick that if all went well in the election there

[1] V. Ranke, *Deutsche Geschichte im Zeitalter der Reformation*, pp. 167 ff.; W. Andreas, *Deutschland vor der Reformation*, pp. 244–55; H. Holborn, *Ulrich von Hutten*, Yale 1937, pp. 10–12.

might be a Cardinal's hat available for one of the Elector's friends! This was the peak of papal accommodation, however, and a new situation was to arise with the formal election of the new Emperor. What with one thing and another, the action against Luther hung fire during the critical spring and summer of 1519. From the Catholic view, it was a fatal delay, and the historian J. Lortz quotes with approval the judgment that nothing could go so far to justify Luther's protest as this subordination of the peril of heresy to the momentary interests of papal and Italian politics.[1]

Two important figures emerge in 1519, the Papal Agent, Charles von Miltitz, and Doctor John Eck, the theologian from Ingolstadt.[2]

Miltitz was that florid sixteenth-century type, an Italianate German with enormous self-confidence, always planning diplomatic gestures on the grand scale which deceived nobody more than himself, a kind of ecclesiastical Von Ribbentrop. Eck was a theologian with a prodigious memory, steeped in scholasticism, skilled in disputations (people did not forget his energetic *Distinguo*). He was also vain, loud-mouthed, violent, a heavy drinker, who according to an unamiable account looked like a butcher—for all the world like the caricature of Luther imagined by some people. Between them their intrigues add a streak of fantasy to the papal strategy in these months: on the one hand, the 'Walrus and Carpenter' tactic of Miltitz (' "I weep for you," the Walrus said, "I deeply sympathize" '); and on the other, the summary 'Off with his head!' of Eck, as the Queen in *Alice*.

Miltitz came over the mountains replenished with polite bribes which ranged from dispensations for Frederick's illegitimate children to the great compliment of the Golden Rose for their devout parent. He brought enough reassuring gossip about the Curia to make Frederick more hopeful about Luther, since the Cardinal Accolti and the Holy Father himself had expressed some trenchant opinions about Tetzel and Prierias, Luther's chief enemies.[3] Miltitz was ready to do all he could to make an

---

[1] J. Lortz, *Reformation in Deutschland*, Freiburg 1948, p. 217.

[2] John Maier of Eck (1486–1543) of the Universities of Heidelberg, Tübingen, Freiburg im Breisgau (D.D. 1510).

[3] Despite R. Bainton (*Church History*, 1947, p. 176) I think Boehmer has the right interpretation of a most confusing passage.

accommodation. He would attend to Tetzel personally, if that would be appreciated. Luther had a series of interviews with Miltitz at Altenburg: he was not at all deceived by the nuncio's slobbering and lachrymose benevolence, but he was willing to refrain from controversy if his opponents would likewise observe an armistice. Miltitz promised to arrange for a more impartial arbitrator—the Archbishop of Salzburg, perhaps, or His Grace of Trier. Luther published a short statement intended to clear away popular misunderstanding of his teaching, and it included two notable paragraphs. The first, 'I have not forbidden good works. I have simply declared that, just as a tree must be good before it can bring forth good fruit, so man must be made good by God's grace before he can do good.'[1]

The other, *On the Roman Church*, must be set within its context. Eck had struck up a friendship with Luther in 1517, and Luther was deeply hurt and angered when Eck circulated among his friends a slashing attack on Luther's Theses. Into this situation leaped the impulsive Karlstadt, and the result was that Eck challenged Karlstadt to a public disputation, though his real objective was Luther. Negotiations for the disputation dragged on for months, and involved a small pamphlet war by way of preliminary. From these preliminary skirmishes a matter arose which was for Luther of catastrophic importance.

In an almost casual aside, in the course of his *Resolutions*, Luther had suggested that, in the time of Gregory I, the Roman Church was not over all other churches (*non erat super alias ecclesias*)[2]. Eck fastened on this in the twelfth of a series of Theses which he published against Karlstadt and Luther. 'We deny that the Roman Church was not superior to other Churches in the time of Sylvester, but we recognize that he who had the seat and faith of blessed Peter has always been the successor of Peter and the Vicar of Christ.'[3]

This was the provocation which turned Luther towards an intensive study of Church History (in the *Historia Tripartita*) and of the Canon Law. In the 'Articles' published after the agreement with Miltitz, the extreme tension of loyalty is apparent. 'The Roman Church,' says Luther, 'is honoured by God above

[1] *Unterricht auf etlich Articckel.* WA 2.69 ff.
[2] WA 1.571.
[3] WA 9.209.40.

all others, by the undoubted fact that SS. Peter and Paul, 46 Popes and many hundreds of thousands of martyrs have shed their blood there . . . if unfortunately there are such things in Rome as might be improved, there neither is, nor can be any reason that one should tear oneself away from the Church in schism. Rather, the worse things become, the more a man should help and cling to her, for by schism and contempt nothing can be mended.'[1]

On March 5th he wrote to Spalatin, 'I was never of a mind to desert the Apostolic See . . . I am quite content that he should be called, and in fact be "Lord". What is that to me? I know that the Grand Turk should be honoured and that he wields his authority by the grace of God, because it is certain that he could have no power unless God willed it.'[2] Here Luther reckons the Papacy as among the 'powers that be' (Rom. 13. 1).

But Eck was a genuine *advocatus diaboli* where Luther was concerned. Luther could not resist capping Eck's twelfth Thesis with his own thirteenth: 'That the Roman Church is superior to all Churches is indeed proved by the far-fetched decrees put out by the Roman pontiffs in the last 400 years. But this ecclesiastical dogma is contrary to the approved histories of 1100 years, the plain teaching of Divine Scripture, and the decree of the Council of Nicea, the most sacred of all councils.' Whatever the effect of this startling view on Luther's enemies, it badly scared all his friends, and Karlstadt and Spalatin, hastily conferring, groaned in apprehension to Luther. He wrote back in vehement annoyance at their temerity: 'Your letter almost made me sick [*ego prope fuissem stomachus motus*—it was probably the truth!], you press me to tell you my plan of campaign . . .'[3] Unwillingly, as though the advertisement of his tactics were tempting Providence, Luther explained that it was really a trap for Eck, that it would certainly entice him into some yet more extravagant thesis, and force him to take up positions from which he could not retract. Subtlety in conflict was not Luther's strong point, and this dangerous game, he was to learn, could be played by others. Meanwhile Luther's appeal to history proceeded, and on March 13th, immersed in study of the Decretals, he wrote: 'And (a word in your ear) I don't know whether the

---

[1] WA 2.72.   [2] WA Br.1.356.8.   [3] WA Br.1.353.1.

Pope is Antichrist himself, or only his apostle, so grievously is Christ, i.e. Truth, manhandled and crucified by him in these decretals.'[1]

The Disputation took place at Leipzig at the beginning of July, 1519 (a day or so before, a fanfare of trumpets had announced in Frankfurt the election of Charles V as Emperor).[2] Duke George had put the Pleissenburg Castle at the disposal of Leipzig University. The Duke was a blunt, honest, rather obtuse prince, something of a Colonel Blimp (witness his remark to Luther—'God's law, or man's law, what's it matter? The Pope's the Pope!') He had been reluctant to allow the intrusion of Luther into what had been arranged as a disputation between Eck and Karlstadt. There was some irritating haggling about this, and about what judges should be appointed, until Luther consented to name the Universities of Erfurt (where he had friends) and Paris (the citadel of the Conciliar view that the Papacy existed 'by human law'). On July 1st Eck, grumbling loudly at the poor quality of the local beer, announced to a friend that the Wittenbergers had arrived. They had come in such numbers (two hundred, to say nothing of dons) that the town hastily armed its Home Guard. The Wittenberg procession was headed by two wagons. The first bore Karlstadt, hugging his beloved text-books, while the second bore the Rector of Wittenberg (Duke Barnim of Pomerania), Luther and Melanchthon. As they entered the gate, the first wagon broke down, depositing Karlstadt heavily in the mud, to the delight of lewd fellows of the baser (Leipzig) sort. But it was a nasty fall, and he hurt his hand and had to be bled, so that what with the injury and the medical treatment he was not in his best form in the succeeding days.

Preliminaries were exhausting. They began at 7 a.m. with a Mass of the Holy Ghost, a new work in twelve parts (and a first performance) by the local musician, George Rhau. There followed a tedious harangue in Latin by Mosellanus on the procedure of debate, and at the end of two long hours the packed audience watched hopefully as the Professor of Poetry subsided, bowing repeatedly, through a back door, only to re-emerge smiling an instant later to introduce more musicians, so

---

[1] WA Br.1.359.29.
[2] K. Brandi, *Kaiser Karl V*, Munich 1941, vol. i, p. 96.

that the hot audience was fain to kneel during a hymn to the Holy Ghost. At long last, came lunch. Later, with the flourishing of trumpets, the disputation began, in courteous, leisurely, mediæval fashion. The first week was spent by Eck and Karlstadt in a debate on the subject of grace and free will. The most lively moment was when an exasperated Eck appealed to the regent whether it was absolutely necessary for Karlstadt to bring all his books with him, and to look up every reference; and, to the relief of most, the decision was in favour of Eck. The debate occupied but part of the day, and there was time for sightseeing. The only positive achievement of Miltitz had been to secure the disgrace of Tetzel, and as he lay dying in Leipzig at this time, Luther sent his enemy a warm and generous word of comfort. By night, a score of heated unofficial disputations waged among the students, under the bright, smoking lights of the taverns and the hostility of the armed watch posted thick about Eck's lodgings.[1]

As the debate continued, the laity found that the entertainment value of a theological disputation on correct and formal lines was soon exhausted. Even some of the theologians preferred to follow the debate with closed eyes, and needed a sad amount of prodding in the intervals. Then, on July 4th, Luther came into the debate and the crowd surged back:

Martin [wrote Mosellanus] is of middle height, of spare body, spent alike with care and study, so that you can almost count his bones: still in the prime of life, with strength undiminished, and a high clear voice.[2]

He began carefully, safeguarding his thirteenth Thesis with the assertion that the Papacy existed by human right (a widespread opinion since the Conciliar movement, and one held by Sir Thomas More in his youth). Danger came, as so often, from the unexpected quarter. In the preliminary correspondence, Eck had flung the epithets 'Hussite' and 'Bohemian' at Luther. But the University of Leipzig had its own historical reasons, and Duke George his own family motives, for being sensitive about Bohemia. Luther had grown up with the normal horror for the

[1] P. Smith, *Luther's Correspondence*, p. 195.
[2] P. Smith, *Luther's Correspondence*, p. 261.

notorious heretic who had been burned at Constance. The pride of the Erfurt Augustinians was John Zachariae, the so-called 'Scourge of Huss', and Luther had often seen the proud tomb on which was carved the Golden Rose awarded to the Augustinian for his zeal.[1] Luther protested vehemently at the charge, but at last his opponent's taunts and this flagrant playing to the gallery got under his guard, and he affirmed that 'among the articles of John Huss and the Hussites which were condemned, are many which are truly Christian and evangelical, and which the Church Universal cannot condemn!' This was sensational! There was a moment of shocked silence, and then an uproar above which could be heard Duke George's disgusted, 'Gad, Sir, that's the Plague!' For Luther had, in fact, moved beyond discussion of the papal power: he had called in question the authority of the great German Council which had so proudly achieved a reunion of the broken Christian world. Eck pressed his advantage home, and Luther, trapped, admitted that since their decrees are also of human law, Councils may err. The rest was anti-climax. Eck could afford to make concessions about Indulgences now that Luther had made this huge admission. Somehow Karlstadt got back into the debate on July 14th, and Duke George hastily closed the proceedings (the Elector of Brandenburg was coming on a hunting visit, and the Saxon Duke must have looked forward to the baying of hounds as a refreshing change from the bellowing of theologians). Once again George Rhau appeared, 'with a hundred pipers and a' and a' ', the Town Musicians, and with an elaborate *Te Deum* the debate concluded. Both sides naturally claimed the victory. It was a tactical success of momentary value for Eck. But the strategic victory was Luther's. Lortz has seen the fatal weakness of the Catholic party in the fact that in the next weeks Eck was entirely preoccupied with his personal success, sunning himself in his new glory, swaggering about the city, culpably heedless of the deep and tragic issues now revealed. Lortz also sees in the refusal of the universities to pronounce judgment against Luther, and the silence of most of them, yet another proof of the genuine theological confusion prevalent in Christendom.[2]

For Luther the debate had been important, for it made him face the implications of his protest. The whole momentum of the

[1] Scheel, ii, p. 64.   [2] J. Lortz, *Reformation*, i, pp. 222-4.

Church struggle was increased by this public attention and by the pamphlet war which flared anew. It gave the final impetus to the hostility of Eck which would lead to Luther's impeachment at Rome. Yet though Eck had secured a triumph, the Leipzig disputation set new forces in motion throughout the German nation. A year hence Eck would be horrified, on returning to Leipzig, at the swift movement of national opinion to Luther's side.[1]

[1] Mackinnon, ii, chap. 5; Charles Beard, *Martin Luther and the Reformation*, London 1896, pp. 289 ff.

CHAPTER SIX

THE REFORMER

'Hear of him! Ay, and I also heard of the molestations, troubles, wars, captivities, cries, groans, frights and fears that he met with, and had in his journey: besides, I must tell you all our country rings with him. There are but few houses that have heard of him and his doings but have sought after and got the records of his pilgrimage.'

THE YEARS 1519–21 saw a prodigious mental activity which drew from Luther a vast, tumultuous flood of ideas, as tracts, treatises, commentaries, polemic, trod on the heels of one another, too fast for three printing presses to keep pace. 'I hold the sword with one hand . . . and with the other build the wall, lest, should I give my whole attention to either pursuit, I should accomplish neither.'[1] In fact, each negative criticism is matched by some positive edification. It is as though the distinction between Wrath and Mercy were reflected in his mind, since his writings fall roughly into those two categories.

He had to meet a vociferous band of polemical opponents, Prierias, Alveldus, Eck, Emser, Catherinus, Cochlaeus, not a man among them of first quality of mind or character. They remind us of Belloc's gibe at Extension Lecturers:

We circulate throughout the Land,
The second rate, and second hand.

But this could not compete with the first-rate and first-hand as it came pouring out of the mind of one of the greatest controversialists of all time. Often he ignored them, and Luther has never received sufficient credit for the books he never wrote. Like Milton, he had a terrible polemical talent, and both enraged their opponents because they could outpace them in vocabulary and verve, and could invariably contrive that last

[1] P. Smith, *Luther's Correspondence*, p. 479.

and rudest word which would be repeated chuckling even among their enemies. For Luther was touched with the comic spirit. His *Answer to the Note of the Stolpen Official*[1] made Miltitz writhe with laughter, and drove Duke George to a series of bellowing guffaws.

He found he could write for common people in the language which they could understand. 'Many people . . . say I write only little pamphlets and German sermons for the unlearned laity. . . . Would to God I had in all my life . . . helped one layman to be better.'[2] It was notoriously a coarsely-spoken age when an English Queen might use language to make the traditional fishwife blush. Anybody who will study Pieter Breughel's conglomeration of Dutch proverbs will realize that a high proportion of the commonplaces of peasant speech would be unmentionable and unprintable in modern polite society. The problem of Luther's language about the Papacy is not of this class, however, and needs more careful treatment than we can give it here, save for the reminder that a similar imagery is to be found in Ezekiel with something of the same psychological motive.[3] By and large, to concentrate, as Grisar had done, all the dirt within a few pages, is to give a completely false impression of Luther as a writer, and even as a polemic divine. And Luther is far removed from the 'Dirt for Dirt's sake' attitude of many of the humanists, and even from the *Merry Tales* which deface the writings of St. Thomas More. This is not at all to deny that Luther's popular polemics reveal him at his worst. Again and again Luther returns to the theme of the Church. It is a misconception to suppose that he fled from reality towards an 'invisible' spiritual Church, or that he preached only an individualist doctrine of Justification. Paul Althaus has suggested that the phrase *communio sanctorum* is one of the keys to his writings in these fateful months, and he loves to expound the solidarity of believers.

Among the heavenly hierarchy, none were object of such popular superstition as the so-called fourteen Auxiliary Saints (SS. Acacius–Vitus) whose combined intercessions covered a grotesque variety of bodily afflictions, and who huddle together on the paintings of a Matthias Grunewald or Lukas Cranach

---

[1] February, 1520. WA 6.135 ff.   [2] WML 1.185.
[3] See the essay 'Dirt' by E. Bevan in *Hellenism and Christianity*.

with moody benevolence. Luther turned instead to the Psalms, to the beautiful *Fourteen of Consolation*, a series of meditations on divine help and spiritual conflict written to comfort Frederick in the illness which overtook him in the late summer of 1519. It is a meditation on the comfort of Christian solidarity—'When we feel pain, suffer, die, let us firmly believe that it is not we, or we alone, but Christ and His Church are in pain, suffering, dying with us. We can apply to ourselves the words of Elisha—"and the Lord opened the eyes of the young man, and he saw: and behold the mountains were full of horses and chariots round about Elisha." This remains for us, too: that is, to pray that our eyes may be opened (the eyes of faith, I mean) that we may see the Church round about us. Then there will be nothing for us to fear.'[1]

Luther wrote his classic tract, *Of Good Works* (1520), at the request of Spalatin. It disproves two common misconceptions, that Luther was not really concerned for morality, and that his doctrine of justification leaves Christian ethics hanging in the air. Luther demonstrates how Christian behaviour derives from the fact that 'the first, the highest and most precious of all good works is faith in Christ'.[2] Faith for Luther is, as in the New Testament, not one of a long agenda of virtues, but a whole dimension of Christian existence, with hope and love the fountain from which the Christian life must spring. The Christian man moves in two worlds: a world which is hid with Christ in God, and the visible, fallen, tangible world where also God has called and placed him. Faith is the point where the Christian unites both worlds,[3] and Luther's doctrine of Temptation (*Anfechtung*) is seen to be the affirmation that the ultimate, un-remitting Christian warfare is this good fight of faith, which comes home to the Christian in the real decision of everyday life. Luther wrote it too quickly, and the tract tails off badly, but the first half is fully occupied with what we have called the dimension of faith. He explains how, from the Christian point of view, it makes all the difference whether good works are done in faith, or apart from it. He uses the effective illustration of a young couple very much in love. 'They make no difference in

---

[1] WML 1.167.   [2] WML 1.187.
[3] See Luther's startling references to faith as a 'mathematical point'. WA 40.3.572.23.

works: they do the great, the long, the much: as gladly as the small, the short, the little, and vice versa: and that too, with joyful, peaceful, confident hearts, and each is a free companion of the other'. The important fact is that they are in love with one another, and whether the young man says it with flowers, with a box of chocolates, with a bus ride, a walk, or a trip to the theatre is a secondary thing. But, adds Luther, 'where there is a doubt, search is made for what is best: then, a distinction of works is imagined, whereby a man may win favour: and yet he goes about with a heavy heart, he is . . . as it were taken captive, more than half in despair, and often makes a fool of himself'.[1] It is when a man is not sure whether his love is returned, that he begins to think quantitively, in terms of bigger and better boxes of chocolates, brighter and more expensive bouquets of flowers, and these assume an altogether different meaning because of the uneasy, unadjusted personal relationship from which they spring. So, says Luther, the Christian does good works 'because it is a pleasure to please God thereby, and he serves God purely and for nothing, content that his service pleases God. On the other hand, he who is not at one with God, or who is in a state of doubts, hunts and worries in what he may do enough, and with many works, to move God'.[2] So, 'Faith must be in all works the master workman, or captain, or they are nothing at all.'[3] And faith is evoked when we turn to Christ. 'Lo, thou must form Christ within thyself, and see how in Him God holds before thee and offers thee His mercy . . . faith therefore does not begin with works, neither do they create it, but it must spring up and flow from the blood, wounds and death of Christ.'[4]

In the second part, Luther expounds the Ten Commandments, beginning with the three Commandments of Love to God. 'See then what a fine golden ring these commandments and their works naturally form, and how from the first commandment and Faith, the second flows into the third, and the third in turn derives from the second into the first. For the first work is to believe, to have a good heart and confidence towards God, the second is to praise God's name, to confess His grace, to give all honour to Him alone. Then follows the third, to worship by praying, hearing God's Word, considering God's benefits,

[1] WML 1.191.   [2] WML 1.191.   [3] WML 1.199.   [4] WML 1.204.

and in addition, chastising oneself and keeping the body under.'[1]

On the fourth Commandment, Luther preaches a homily on obedience in the home, which speaks to the condition of sixteenth- and twentieth-century indiscipline, and he expands it to cover obedience to 'the spiritual mother, the Holy Christian Church', and the temporal rulers. There are two memorable sentences. The first, Luther's conviction that 'there is not such great danger in the Temporal power as in the Spiritual when it does wrong . . . for the temporal power has nothing to do with preaching and with faith and with the first three commandments. But the spiritual power does harm, not only when it does wrong, but also when it neglects its own duty and engages in other things, even if they were better than the very best works of the temporal power. Therefore we must resist it when it does not do right, and not resist the temporal power although it does wrong'.[2]

The second is the famous picture of the Ruler as the 'Mad Coachman', a stern warning to all rulers, courts and courtiers, 'for when a Prince rules after his own mad will and follows his own opinion, he is like a mad coachman who rushes straight ahead with horse and wagon, through bushes, briars, ditches, water, up hill and down dale, regardless of roads or bridges: he will not drive long, for all will crash in ruin'.[3]

Luther expounds the other Commandments in company with most sixteenth-century moralists, deploring luxury, gluttony, litigiousness, chicanery and brawling, and he adds a sufficiently modern comment: 'The trouble is, there is no real government in the world. No one wants to work, and therefore the mechanics must give their workers holidays: then they are free, and nobody can tame them.'[4] Those who have accused Luther of writing down the Sermon on the Mount in terms of the Ten Commandments will find that the reverse is the case, and that here there is a powerful presentation of the Commandments in terms of the magisterial command of love, which springs from faith in Christ.

[1] WML 1.249.   [2] WML 1.263.

[3] WML 1.265. For a fine modern Lutheran exposition see Eivvind Berggrav's address *Wenn der Kutscher Trunken ist* (illegally circulated in 1941); E. Berggrav, *Der Staat und Der Mensch*, Stockholm 1946, pp. 365 ff.

[4] WML 1.267.

'Again you see that faith must be the master workman . . . so entirely are all works comprised in faith.'[1]

Luther's relations with the humanists are complex. In Erfurt, their circle was formed after his profession, but its members included some of his former undergraduate friends, and when he took his Plautus and Virgil with him into the monastery he must have had some thought of continuing classical studies. He shared the humanist concern for 'good letters' (*bonæ litteræ*) and also their second objective 'sacred letters' (*sacræ litteræ*) in the more restricted sense of the search for more accurate texts and editions of the Bible and of the Fathers. We know how eagerly he turned to the latest critical tools, to Le Fevre's edition of the Psalms, to Reuchlin's Hebrew Dictionary, to the New Testament of Erasmus, and how he used them for the basis of his own lectures. He worked hard at Greek in the next years and acquired a working knowledge of Hebrew. In yet a third direction, he was at one with the humanists, in their opposition to late scholasticism and the demand for simplification of studies in the schools, a demand such as, in the sixteenth century, joined Sir Thomas More and William Tyndale, Stephen Gardiner and Robert Barnes, Erasmus, Luther, Hutten. In the Reuchlin controversy, in which the great Hebraist was attacked by the Dominicans, and a combined menace of anti-Semitism and obscurantism brought a distinguished career to misery and ruin, Luther was unreservedly on the side of Reuchlin. Yet there is a difference. The humanists were greatly given to anonymous writing, and to satire, to a gifted mockery which acted as a dangerously negative corrosive to popular opinion. Luther distrusted the brilliant obscenities of the *Letters of the Obscure Men* which set the world laughing at Reuchlin's enemies, and later, the *Antibarbari* and the *Praise of Folly* of Erasmus, not least because he felt the times demanded tears rather than laughter.

Luther was primarily a theologian and preacher, not an academic. Europe owes an enormous debt to the humanist bookworms who loved the very feel of a book, who tracked down manuscripts across the continent, who appreciated the differences of type and who set a high value (witness the lovely handwriting of Erasmus and Sir John Cheke) on fine penman-

[1] WML 1.284.

ship. Luther had no time for such preoccupations. He was early sensible of a difference between his theological beliefs and theirs. Their catchword, the 'renaissance of Christ', was alien to his way of thinking. In a letter about Erasmus in 1516,[1] and again in 1518, he put the difference between them in shrewd and penetrating criticism: it was, in effect, the same contrast as between Jerome and Augustine. It was a pity that Spalatin passed on the criticism without softening it at all, for Erasmus was thin-skinned. But with the opening of the Church conflict, Luther found he needed all the support he could get, and he corresponded with almost all the leading members of the humanist circles in the great universities and cities, Erfurt, Heidelberg, Nuremberg, Strassburg, Basel. This need for support, and the softening influence of Melanchthon (the lifelong friend and correspondent of Erasmus) may account for the warmth of Luther's letter to the humanist in March, 1519:[2] 'Who is there whose inmost being Erasmus has not penetrated, whom Erasmus does not reach, in whom Erasmus does not reign? . . . wherefore, dear Erasmus, learn to love this insignificant brother also [*Fraterculus*—the rankling epithet of Cajetan]: he is assuredly your most zealous friend.'

Erasmus sent a polite reply, not too cordial, for this kind of semi-private correspondence was bound to get printed sooner or later after it had gone the rounds. That criss-cross of correspondence provided this intelligentsia with the faint premonition of the modern quarterly review, so that the sixteenth century is littered with tiffs and broken friendships over real or imaginary breaches of confidence. As Luther moved out into public controversy, the admiration of the humanists deepened, the more so as they found it difficult to get full information about his doctrines. 'About Luther there is no really certain news,' wrote Beatus Rhenanus to the eager enquiry of his Swiss friend, Ulrich Zwingli, in 1518. And among this circle it was agreed that Luther was the embodiment of their ideal of a Christian (*homo vere Christi imaginem referens*), a mixture of Hercules and David! As Luther's troubles deepened, and public condemnation became imminent, they grew more wary. Zwingli had his own troubles to get along with, but his biographers have had to note the striking fact that,

[1] WA Br.1.70.　　[2] WA Br.1.361.

though he bought most of Luther's tracts in 1519, none of them bears a single comment in Zwingli's own hand, who was otherwise wont to cover his margins with his jottings. And in July, 1520, Zwingli could write pointedly: 'I read almost nothing of Luther nowadays.'[1]

Erasmus, writing to Albert of Mainz (November, 1519) said: 'Luther is as unknown to me as anybody, nor have I yet had time to read his works, except that I have glanced at them hastily.'[2] In September, 1520, he wrote even more circumspectly to the Pope: 'I do not know Luther, nor have I read his books, except ten or twelve pages, and those hastily.'[3]

In the pamphlet war which broke out in 1519, the humanists took a manful share, and produced the famous *Eccius Dedolatus* (Mr. Corner Polished Off!) which set Germany laughing at Luther's most formidable opponent. But Erasmus did Luther better service than the Reformer knew. In part, this was a struggle between generations, and Erasmus now belonged to an older period of humanism, and had now to watch the young men turn more and more away from his spiritual leadership— Zwingli, Bucer, Melanchthon, Oecolampadius were all Erasmians turned Reformer. If Erasmus could have understood Luther's doctrines he would have preferred his smooth and rounded 'philosophy of Christ'. He was not by temperament a fighter, and he found himself in a moving situation not at all to his liking where the things he cared most for were placed in jeopardy.[4]

Though there was much about Luther he disliked and deplored, he would never condemn him outright and altogether, and he hated with all his heart the blind obscurantism which had dogged him from his youth, had ruined Reuchlin, and now closed on Luther. 'The chiefs of the Dominican monastery have acted in ... a disgraceful way. One of their number said in the hearing of some laymen, 'Would that I could fasten my teeth in

[1] A. Rich, *Die Anfänge der Theologie Huldrych Zwingli*, Zurich 1949, pp. 73 ff.; O. Farner, *H. Zwingli*, Zurich 1946, pp. 334 ff.

[2] P. Smith, *Luther's Correspondence*, p. 238 (No. 192).

[3] P. Smith, *Luther's Correspondence*, p. 355 (No. 297).

[4] K. A. Meissinger, *Erasmus*, 1948; M. M. Philipps, *Erasmus and the Northern Renaissance*, London 1950; Renaudet, *Études Erasmiennes*, Paris 1939; R. Stupperich, *Der Humanismus und die Wiedervereinigung der Konfessionen* (Ver. Ref. Ges.), Leipzig 1936; Huizinga, *Erasmus;* P. S. Allen, *Age of Erasmus;* P. Smith, *Erasmus*.

Luther's throat: I should not fear to go to the Lord's Supper with his blood on my mouth.'[1]

At a time when the theologians of Louvain and Cologne were enraged against him, when the Papal Nuncio was reporting that Erasmus was worse than Luther, Erasmus had an important interview with the Elector Frederick at Cologne (November, 1520). The scholar's well-planted anti-clerical epigrams were too subtle for the Saxon, and he was annoyed by his evasiveness. But if Erasmus had thrown the weight of his reputation against Luther then it might have been serious. As it was, the Elector persisted until he obtained the promise from the young Emperor that Luther should not be condemned unheard (*nisi auditus*).

Erasmus was the patriarch of cosmopolitan humanism: Ulrich von Hutten of the ardent nationalism of the German scholars. Like Erasmus, the flitting Dutchman, Hutten was a wandering scholar (he abandoned the monastery in the year in which Luther made his profession) darting from university to university like a restless dragonfly, penning poems and satires, plotting politics and brawling with Italians in their taverns, truculently mingling braggadocio with sentimentalism—a recognizable type and uncomfortably modern. He was a mixture of academic, politician and fanatic (the Sir Harry Vane of the German Reformation?). In Hutten we link Luther not only with humanism, but with the political fate of Germany. Constitutionally, Germany was to defy all amendment: the entail of centuries of division and conflict, exacerbated by the tension of Pope and Emperor, was too intricate, and the divisions between Emperor (imperial and dynastic interests) and Princes, the Knights, the cities and the towns, and the tradesmen and peasants, were deep clefts.[2] There could be no such alliance between royalty and gentry as in England would produce a Reformation Parliament, or between the gentry and the boroughs as could achieve the Elizabethan House of Commons. Amid a tangle of jurisdictions and sovereignties, the knights of Germany lived in a brutal world, on the fringe of the economic and social revolution, the veneer of chivalry worn thin, the prey to family feuds and mutual brigandage. Yet there was

---

[1] P. Smith, *Luther's Correspondence*, p. 376 (from Erasmus).
[2] Gerhard Ritter, *Luther: Gestalt und Tat*, Munich 1949, p. 70 ff.

indubitably a surging life and a great weight of frustrated aspiration. For a moment it seemed that the knights might have found leaders in Hutten and his politically-minded chief, Von Sickingen, for a fleeting interval as though the young Emperor might achieve the unity of the German nation. For a few months it seemed that Martin Luther himself, 'the hero of the German nation', might fuse the whole people in a national revival out of which it might find independence and equilibrium of soul. Luther's writings of 1520, with their appeal to national feeling, may be playing to the gallery (it was more than this, for it was his own deep German emotion), but at least the gallery was there, crowded, excited, vociferous.

The attempts of Miltitz (continued throughout 1519) to quench the conflagration only created, from the Saxon point of view, a useful amount of smoke. But at the end of the year Eck sent a formidable, documented indictment to Rome. Early in 1520 the Universities of Louvain and Cologne prepared a detailed condemnation of Luther's doctrines and forwarded their report to the Curia. The Pope appointed a formal commission. The first (February 1st) was soon dissolved, since even the Cardinals Cajetan (theologian) and Accolti (canonist) could not ensure a judicious report. The second (February 11th) made a wise attempt to discriminate between Luther's heretical articles and those 'scandalous and offensive to pious ears'. Then Eck arrived, and the upshot was a third commission and the Papal Bull (signed June 15th) *Exsurge Domine*—'Arise, O God and judge Thine own cause . . . the wild boar has broken into the vineyard . . .' It condemned forty-one articles, but did not name Luther, and was content to append an evangelical 'Monition' to him, giving him time to recant. Eck and Aleander were appointed to bring the Bull to the cities of South and North Germany. They were horrified to find how swiftly public opinion was moving to the side of Luther. In the scene of former triumph, Leipzig, Eck was openly menaced in the streets, and had to take refuge with the Dominicans, while he had the indignity of knowing that his servants were manhandled severely, soon after their master had scampered to a safer place.

Miltitz made a last attempt to retrieve the situation and his waning reputation, and he saw Luther who agreed to write a last letter to the Pope, and, even now, to make an armistice with his opponents. Luther wrote the letter and despatched it with a copy of his little book, *The Liberty of a Christian Man*. But in the last weeks his own mind had fatefully and decisively hardened.

The letters between Luther and Spalatin reveal the stress within the Reformer's mind and the attempt of the latter to act as a brake upon his leader's impetuosity. 'Let there be a new and great conflagration,' answered Luther, 'who can resist the counsel of God? Who knows whether these insensate men are not predestined by Him as the means of revealing the truth? . . . God alone is in this business. We are carried away by Him. We are led rather than lead.'[1]

'I beg of you, if you have a right feeling for the Gospel, do not think this matter can be carried through without tumult, scandal, or sedition . . . this is God's war, who did not come to bring peace . . . you ought to beware of thinking that Christ will achieve things in the earth quietly and softly, when you see that he fought with his own blood, and afterwards all the martyrs.'[2] Since the Leipzig disputation he had been in touch with some Bohemian humanists and he now read the Huss-Wycliffite *De Ecclesia*. He told Spalatin, 'I have been teaching all that John Huss taught unawares, and so has Staupitz. In short, we are all Hussites, though we have not known it, even Paul and Augustine.'[3]

He firmly opposed Spalatin's temerity. 'Good God . . . I wrote you before not to presume that this matter has been begun or wrought in your, my, or anybody's decision and action; if it is of God, its bounds are far against, beyond, above, below, your and my comprehension.'[4] But he admits his own weakness. 'I cannot deny that I am more violent than is befitting,' and then he growls, 'those who know this ought to beware of baiting the dog!'[5] He read Hutten's edition and exposure of the *Donation of Constantine*, and in his present mood the effect was devastating. 'Good God, how great is the darkness and iniquity of these Romans . . . I am so horrified that I have hardly any doubt left (*prope non dubitem*) that the Pope is that very Antichrist himself which the common report expects, so well do all the things he lives, does, speaks, ordains, fit the picture.'[6]

[1] WA Br.2.39.9–12.21.   [2] WA Br.2.41–3.   [3] WA Br.2.42.2.22
[4] WA Br.2.43.   [5] WA Br.2, *ibid.* 1.65.   [6] WA Br.2.48.22.

In May, the Franciscan, Alveldus, published a trenchant writing asserting the divine origin of the Papal Primacy, and Luther wrote rapidly a tract which was in print by June. He does not deny the reality of the visible Church, but he finds its essence in an assembly of persons, the external marks of the Church being 'Baptism, the Sacrament, and the Gospel: not Rome, or this place, or that'.[1] Over this Church Jesus Christ Himself rules actively, and presently 'Christ is the Head and He ruleth alone'.[2]

During these weeks Luther reached a turning point in this thought about the Roman Church. He wrote these final words: 'Farewell, unhappy, hopeless, blasphemous Rome! The Wrath of God hath come upon thee, as thou deservest. We have cared for Babylon, and she is not healed: let us then, leave her, that she may be the habitation of dragons, spectres and witches, and true to her name of Babel, an everlasting confusion, a new pantheon of wickedness.'[3] The result was the writing of the three revolutionary manifestos of the summer of 1520. It is a clue to Luther's character that in these very weeks, when serious student riots broke out in Wittenberg over internal matters between town and gown, Luther himself was on the side of authority, and preached publicly to the students on the duty of obedience, thereby winning a good deal of unpopularity, and the threat of physical violence from the ringleaders.

Luther was fortunate in finding superb titles for his tracts. The first, *An Open Letter to the Christian Nobility of the German Nation concerning the reform of the Christian Estate*, is the real manifesto. It is an appeal to the leaders of Germany, to the young Emperor, to the Princes and the Knights, and to the great Imperial Cities. It begins with a solemn warning to the leaders of the people that they must never imagine they can achieve the amendment of Christendom by might of arms. 'We must go to work despairing of physical force, and humbly trusting God,' for 'we are not dealing with men, but with the princes of hell, who can fill the world with war and bloodshed, but whom war and bloodshed do not overcome.'[4] Luther begins by describing the three walls of the Romanists: their claim to possess jurisdiction superior to that of the temporal power, their claim to

---

[1] WML 1.361.   [2] WML 1.357.   [3] WA 6.329.   [4] WML 2.64.

have the sole power to interpret Scripture, and the papal claim to have sole authority to call a general council.[1]

Much of the pamphlet is not original, for it consists of widely aired grievances of the German people, the kind of abuses and exactions about which Duke George was as vehement as his brother ruler, the Elector. More striking is the theological ground of Luther's appeal. He enunciates the doctrine that fundamentally there is only one Christian estate (*Stand*) though Christians may be called to fulfil a different office (*Amt*). That estate is that ultimate situation in which as sinners we are accepted by God for Christ's sake, and in consequence there is a priesthood common to all believers, in virtue of their baptism and their Christian faith. In spiritual things this fundamental priesthood involves equality, so that when a bishop is chosen, it is as though 'ten brothers, all kings' sons and equal heirs, were to choose one of themselves to rule the inheritance for them all . . . they would all be kings and equal in power, though one of them would be charged with the duty of ruling'.[2]

Nevertheless, Luther establishes an important principle when he continues: 'No one must put himself forward, and undertake, without our consent and election, to do what is in the power of all of us. For what is common to all, no one dare take upon himself without the will and the command of the community.'[3] This raises the important question of the ground on which Luther asks the secular authorities to intervene in the desperate state of Christendom and to take the initiative in calling a free, Christian council. Luther had no naïve and exaggerated optimism about the rulers of Germany: that 'a prince is a rare bird in heaven', and that power corrupts, are affirmations we can find at all levels and all periods of Luther's writings, from his *Romans* (1515) to *Genesis* (1540). But, as we have already seen, Luther regarded the abuse of spiritual power as far more deadly than that of the temporal power. He is writing, moreover, in an emergency situation, in which the Church has failed to obtain reform from the spiritual authorities who have become themselves an obstacle to amendment.

In this case, reform becomes the common concern of the whole Christian estate. In this emergency, the persons most fit to intervene on behalf of all are the secular authorities, since it

[1] WML 2.65.   [2] *ibid*. 67.   [3] *ibid*. 68.

is their God-entrusted office (*Amt*) to wield the sword of government and administration, and to protect the whole community.[1]
'Therefore when necessity demands, the first man who is able
should as a faithful member of the whole body, do what he can
to bring about a truly free council.' 'No one can do this
as well as the temporal authorities, especially since they also
are fellow Christians, fellow priests.'[2] If a fire breaks out in a
city, it is the duty of each citizen to act in the emergency,
'. . . how much more in the spiritual city of Christ, if a fire of
offence breaks out'.

   Here again is Luther's insistence on the active, present rule of
Christ. 'For Christ in heaven . . . needs no Vicar, but He sits
and sees, does and knows all things, and has all authority.'[3] In
one sense the tract belongs to a vast literature concerning the
spiritual and temporal powers: in another it is symptomatic of
the sixteenth-century emphasis on the 'godly Prince'; yet
Luther's appeal is grounded in his theology, and again and
again includes stern warnings of the perils and limitations of all
earthly power. 'Ah! well, for the Lord God it is a small thing to
toss empires and principalities to and fro! He is so generous with
them, that once in a while he gives a kingdom to a knave, and
takes it from a good man.'[4] 'All do as they please . . . and the
government is of as much use as if it did not exist . . . O what a
rare bird will a lord or ruler be in heaven.'[5] Luther concludes:
'I think I have pitched my song in too high a key, and have
made too many proposals . . . have attacked too many things
sharply . . . but what am I to do? I am in duty bound to speak
. . . I prefer the wrath of the world to the Wrath of God: they
can do no more than take my life.'[6] By the end of August, copies
were circulating in thousands all over Germany. 'Few writings
of Luther have had comparable effect upon German public
opinion.'[7]

   'I know another little song about Rome . . . I will sing that,
too, and pitch the notes to the top of the scale.'[8] Luther fulfilled
the threat in his Latin treatise, intended for the humanists and

[1] K. Holl, 'Luther und das Landesherrliche Kirchenregiment', *Ges.
Aufs., Luther*, p. 326 ff.
[2] WML 2.78.   [3] WML 2.109.   [4] WML 2.155.   [5] WML 2.163.
[6] WML 2.164.
[7] 'Martin Luther', *Werke*, Munich 1948, vol. ii, pp. 391–2.
[8] WML 2.164.

for the clergy, *A Prelude on the Babylonian Captivity of the Church.*
It had grown immediately under the impulse of a series of fierce
attacks upon him ('they cling to me like mud to a wheel'), but it
also embodies the full implications of his decision against Rome,
and he announced its publication to Spalatin at the same time
as he reports the arrival of Eck with the Papal Bull.[1] Luther
declares, 'I must deny that there are seven sacraments and hold
for the present to but three—baptism, penance, and the bread.'[2]
Much of the treatise is a compilation from other writings of the
last months. The writing was bound to shock clerical opinion, if
only for its revolutionary attack on the doctrine of transubstantiation and upon the sacrifice of the Mass. More
positively there is a development of his doctrine of the Word,
and a full position of the Sacrament of Baptism, which restores
the eschatological significance of its symbolism. 'Just as the
truth of this divine promise, pronounced over us, continues
until death, so our faith in the same ought never to cease,
but be nourished and strengthened until death, by the
continual remembrance of this promise made to us in our
baptism.'[3]

'When we rise from sins or repent, we do but return to the
power and faith of the baptism from whence we fell, and find
our way back to the promise then made to us.'[4] 'Baptism signifies two things—death and resurrection: that is, full and
complete justification.'[5] 'Therefore, whether by penance or by
any other way, you can only return to the power of your
baptism.' 'We therefore are never without the sign of baptism,
nor yet without the thing it signifies: nay, we must be baptized
more and more completely until we perfectly fulfil the sign, at
the last day.'[6] 'For we are indeed, little children, continually
baptized anew in Christ.'[7] That Christianity is no legalism is
affirmed: 'Neither Pope nor Bishop nor any other man has a
right to impose a syllable of law upon a Christian man without
his consent,[8] although 'I admit that Christians ought to bear
this accursed tyranny as they would bear any other violence.'[9]
Underlying the exposition of the Sacraments is Luther's theme
of the Word: 'The Church owes its life to the Word of promise,

---

[1] WA Br.2.191 (October 30th, 1520).   [2] WML 2.177.   [3] *ibid.* 221.
[4] WML 2.221.   [5] *ibid.* 230.   [6] *ibid.* 232.   [7] *ibid.* 236.
[8] WML 2.233.   [9] *ibid.* 234.

and is nourished and preserved by this same Word—the promises of God make the Church, not the Church the promises of God.'[1]

The Priesthood of All Believers again appears, but this time to make plain that there must be a regular ministry: 'We are all priests . . . we have the same power in respect of the Word and all the Sacraments. However, no one may make use of this power, except by the consent of the community, or by the call of a superior.'[2] Luther concludes that, properly speaking, there are two sacraments (promises of God, with signs attached to them) 'Baptism and Bread, for only in these two do we find both the divinely instituted sign and the promise of the forgiveness of sins'.[3] Luther emphasizes, in the case of the Sacrament of the Altar, as in the case of Baptism, the eschatological character of the sacrament: 'For the bread is truly the sacrament of dying: for in it we commemorate the passing of Christ out of this world, that we may imitate Him.'[4]

Luther's *Of the Liberty of a Christian Man*[5] belongs to the writings of Mercy rather than of Wrath, yet there is an inner connection, in doctrine with the other two tracts, and though it treats the relation between God and the individual soul it is plain that Luther thinks of this within the solidarity of the Church. The little book continues the theme of the sermon *Of Good Works* in expounding the life of faith. The opening words strike the theme: 'What great virtue there is in Faith.'[6] Luther enunciates the famous paradox:

A Christian Man is a free lord over all things, and
    subject to none.
A Christian Man is a bounden servant of all things,
    and servant of all.

He explains that man has a 'twofold nature, a spiritual and bodily' (II Cor. 4. 16). But this dualism is explained in biblical, not Platonic, terms, as the antagonism of 'flesh 'and 'spirit'

---

[1] WML 2.273.   [2] *ibid.* 283.   [3] *ibid.* 291–2.   [4] *ibid.* 292.
[5] Luther, *Werke*, Munich ed. 1948, 2.269 ff; R. Will, *La Liberté Chrétienne*, Strasbourg, 1922; Runestam, *Den Kristliga Friheten*, p. 11 ff.
[6] WML 2.312.

(Gal. 5. 17).[1] No external righteousness whatever can 'produce Christian righteousness or liberty' for the Christian: but on the other hand, no affliction or persecution or outward peril can hurt the 'clear conscience'.[2]

For this, one thing, and one thing alone, is needful—the Word of God. 'The soul can do without all things except the Word of God . . . if it has the Word it is rich and lacks nothing, since this Word is the Word of life, of truth, of light, of peace, of righteousness, of salvation, of joy, of liberty.'[3] This was the supreme ministry for which Christ was sent. 'The Word is the Gospel of God concerning His Son . . . for to preach Christ means to feed the soul, to make it righteous, to set it free and to save it, if it believe the preaching.' Through this faith 'you may become a new man, in that all your sins are forgiven, and are justified by the merits of another, namely, of Christ alone'.[4] Scripture is divided into Law and Promise, and the law teaches a man his own weakness . . . then being truly humbled and reduced to nothing in his own eyes, he finds in himself no means of justification and salvation.'[5] But when he turns to the promises of God he finds 'that the soul which clings to them with a firm faith, is so united with them, nay, altogether taken up into them, that it not only shares in all their power, but is saturated and made drunk with it . . . if a touch of Christ healed . . . how much more will this most tender touch of the Spirit, this absorbing of the Word, communicate to the soul all things that are the Word's'.[6] For 'in the soul, faith alone and the Word hold sway. As the Word is, so it makes the soul, as heated iron glows like fire because of the union of the fire with it'.[7] 'This is that Christian liberty which does not indeed cause us to live in idleness or in wickedness, but makes the law and works unnecessary for any man's righteousness and salvation.'[8]

This faith is 'in all things most obedient to God'. 'It unites the soul with Christ as a bride united with her bridegroom . . . nay, human marriages are but frail types of this one true marriage.'[9] Thus the believing soul can claim 'whatever Christ has as if it

---

[1] Runestam, 11.   [2] WML 2.313.   [3] ibid. 314.   [4] ibid. 315.
[5] ibid. 317.   [6] ibid. 318.
[7] ibid. 318; Runestam, 12: 'Word and faith, these constitute Christian liberty.'
[8] WML 2.319.   [9] ibid. 320.

were her own, and whatever the soul has, Christ claims as His own'. In an important sentence, Luther shows that this is no mystic quietism, for it is union with Christ in death and resurrection 'not only of communion, but of a blessed strife and victory, salvation and redemption'.[1] Christ 'by the wedding-ring of faith shares in the sins, death and pains of hell which are His bride's, nay, makes them His own, and acts as if they were His own, and as if He himself had sinned: He suffered, died and descended into Hell that He might overcome them all'.[2] Faith, then, is no mystic 'abandonment' (*Gelassenheit*) but the appropriation of this 'mighty duel' in which Jesus Christ has conquered sin, death and the devil. Luther goes straight from this thought to that of the Priesthood of All Believers, and it is plain that the heart of the doctrine for him lies in no individualist conception of private judgment, or the denial of priesthood altogether, but rather that solidarity of Christian communion expressed in the ministry of intercession: 'As priests we are worthy to appear before God to pray for others, and to teach one another the things of God.'[3]

The believing Christian has an immovable source of peace and joy. 'Who would have power to harm such a heart, or make it afraid?'[4] In the second part of his treatise, Luther turns to the outward man, and begins by denouncing those who misunderstand the teaching of the New Testament or abuse it by crying: ' "We will take our ease and do no works, and be content with faith." I answer: "Not so, ye wicked men, not so. As long as we live in the flesh we only begin and make some progress in that which shall be perfected in the future life." '[5] But in this life, the justified man 'must needs govern his own body and have dealings with men', even though 'it is his own occupation to serve God joyfully and for naught, in a love that is unconstrained'. His works do not justify him, 'but he does them out of spon-

---

[1] WML 2.321.
[2] *ibid.* 321.
[3] It is noteworthy that Dr. Asmussen's profound exposition of the theological grounds for the famous 'Guilt Declaration' of the German Evangelical Church (October, 1945) with its conception of Christian solidarity, is grounded in this doctrine of the Priesthood of Believers. WML 2.325.
[4] WML 2.327.
[5] *ibid.* 328.

taneous[1] love in obedience to God and considers nothing save
the approval of God, whom he would in all things most
scrupulously obey'. The Christian man 'does all that he does
out of pure liberty and freely'. 'We should devote all our works
to the welfare of others, since each has such abundant riches in
his faith, that all his other works, and his whole life, are a
surplus with which he can by voluntary benevolence serve and
do good to his neighbour.'[2] 'Why should I not then freely, joyfully, with all my heart and an eager will do all things which I
know are pleasing and acceptable to such a Father . . . I will
therefore give myself as a Christ to my neighbour, just as Christ
offered Himself to me.'[3] Thus love flows from the relationship
with God through faith, and from the love of God to us flows
our love for our fellows. 'From faith flow love and joy in the
Lord, and from love a joyful, willing and free mind that serves
one's neighbour willingly and takes no account of gratitude or
ingratitude, praise or blame, of gain or loss.'[4] This love makes
us 'free, joyful, almighty workers and conquerors over all tribu-
lations, servants of our neighbours, and yet lords of all'. For this
is the ground of the Christian ethic, 'as our Heavenly Father
has in Christ freely come to our help, so we ought freely to help
our neighbour through the body and its works, and each should
become as it were a Christ to the other, that we may be Christs
to one another, and Christ may be the same in all, that we may
be truly Christians'.[5] For this it is to be a Christian man: 'We
are so named after Christ not because He is absent from us, but
because He dwells in us, that is because we believe in Him and
are Christs to one another, and do to our neighbours as Christ
does to us.'[6]

'We conclude, therefore, that a Christian man lives not in
himself, but in Christ and his neighbour. Otherwise he is not a
Christian. He lives in Christ by faith, and in his neighbour
through love. By faith he is caught up beyond himself into God,

---

[1] Luther's stress on the spontaneity of Christian obedience is important
for the understanding of his ethic (and to be remembered against his
doctrine of the 'Bondage of the Will' of the unredeemed). 'This doctrine of
the freedom of real moral action is the central thought in Luther's ethic'
(E. Sormunen, *Die Eigenart der Lutherischen Ethik*, Helsinki 1938, p. 36; see
also G. Wingren, *Luthers lära om Kallelsen*, Lund 1948, pp. 105 ff.)

[2] WML 2.336.   [3] *ibid.* 337.   [4] *ibid.* 338.   [5] *ibid.* 338.
[6] *ibid.* 339.

by love he sinks down beneath himself into his neighbour: yet he always remains in God, and in His love.'[1]

Its fine title has perhaps caused its exaltation above the *Of Good Works* in repute, but taken together the two tracts form a coherent exposition of the ethic of faith and hope and love, which, as in the New Testament, links the whole Christian life with the drama of salvation, with the death and resurrection of Christ's 'mighty duel', and with a perfect and sufficient righteousness freely available in Him apprehended here and now through faith, hope and love. When the burning fire of the *Christian Nobility* had gone, and the earthquake of the *Babylonian Captivity* had ceased to quiver, there succeeded this still, small voice, more gentle than the dark apocalyptic background could presage, the sweet reasonableness (*epieikia*) not of Aristotle, but of Christ.

Rumours reached Luther of the progress of the papal nuncios, of the burning of his books in one city after another (but always with some counter-demonstration, and often with the secret substitution of other books!). Then, on December 10th, was enacted the solemn scene which Lord Acton saw as the true inauguration of the Reformation. Near the Elster Gate in Wittenberg, a fire was kindled by Agricola, and into the smoke were cast the volumes of the Canon Law, the Papal Decretals, and the *Summa Angelica* of Angelo of Chiavasso. That Luther should single out the Canon Law is significant, and is a comment not so much on the gallant attempt of the great lawyer popes of the fourteenth and fifteenth centuries to spin a legal way out of the web in which they were involved, as on Luther's mental pilgrimage. He saw in these books, says Boehmer, 'the confusion of law with religion, of the kingdom of the world with the Kingdom of God, of politics with the cure of souls, of legalism with piety, and the secularization which is the necessary consequence of such confusion . . . the *Summa Angelica* served as a typical example of how far the cure of souls had been led astray by this profane botching of religion'.[2]

Suddenly, Luther himself stepped out from among the doctors and, deeply agitated, consigned a small volume to the rising

[1] WML 2.342.
[2] Boehmer, *Road to Reformation*, p. 376.

flames. His words of imprecation were but faintly heard, and many could hardly have known that he had burned the Papal Bull against himself. The group stared at the red flames, burning brightly in the winter air. Then, somebody broke the tense silence, and the professors and doctors edged and elbowed their serious way out of the crowd. The undergraduates remained for rough sport and foolery, at an occasion which gave them more than usual scope for noisy demonstration.

CHAPTER SEVEN

THE KNIGHT OF FAITH

'GREATHEART: *And did none of these things discourage you?*
VALIANT FOR TRUTH: *No, they seemed as so many nothings
to me.*
GREATHEART: *Then this was your victory, even your faith.*
VALIANT FOR TRUTH: *It was so. I believed, and therefore
came out, got into the way, fought all that set themselves
against me, and by believing am come to this place.*'

THE LUTHERAN AFFAIR was a graver danger than the Curia
could be made to realize, and this accounts for the hysterical
intensity of Aleander's despatches to Rome, in which he tried
vainly to shock the authorities beyond the Alps into apprehension of the ferment moving distant Germany. For the Church
was fighting a new war with the weapons of a bygone age. As
the papal nuncios had moved from town to town with their
stock of Bulls (Eck had the levity to employ them for purposes of
personal vendetta, adding his own enemies' names to that of
Luther), they might wrangle, browbeat, plead with the authorities
to post the Bull. But if they succeeded, like as not it was torn
down overnight, to be replaced with some insolent scurrility
against the Pope. The pamphlets of Hutten and Luther, and
broadsheets bearing their pictures side by side, streamed out in
their thousands, and, despite all the papal controversialists,
kept the firm initiative. Papal diplomacy vainly hoped that
the old diplomatic tricks could succeed against the deep
earnestness of men who cared only to buy truth. The
letters of Aleander openly confess the failure of his attempt to
win allies by bribery and lying, but for every man amenable to
papal intrigue, there was a dozen, even among the worldly
nobles, who caught the heady infection of national indignation
and pent-up anti-clerical resentment. Aleander complained
bitterly to his masters. He who liked to do himself well (a
popular academic turned diplomat liked his little comforts)

found to his chagrin that, wherever he went, hotels became mysteriously full, rooms engaged, and that his money was refused with contempt, until in mid-winter he had to shiver without a fire in the dingiest room, overlooking the dank mists of Father Rhine. He tried to warm himself with epithets against Luther, 'this Mohammed', 'this Arius', this 'Son of Satan', but he had to confess: 'The whole of Germany is in full revolt: nine-tenths raise the war cry "Luther!", while the watchword of the other tenth who are indifferent to Luther is "Death to the Roman Curia".'[1]

On the one hand the indifference and ignorance at the Curia: on the other, political intrigue about the Emperor. Of the orthodox intentions of Charles V there was never any doubt. He deliberately and publicly tore up Luther's *Appeal*, and ventured to rebuke the powerful Von Sickingen for speaking well of Luther in his presence. But between the person of the Emperor and the Imperial Mandate stood formidable vested interests, including his own advisers, Chièvres and Gattinara, and his wily confessor, Glapion. The forthcoming Diet would be a delicate matter, and the Emperor could ill afford to antagonize any powerful party. He promised the Elector Frederick that Luther should come under a safe conduct. But the publication (January 3rd, 1521) of a Papal Bull of excommunication against Luther strengthened Aleander's attempt to upset the project, for in his despatch he put a firm finger on the disadvantage from the papal standpoint of a public hearing for Luther at Worms. 'If he did not recant, and on account of his safe conduct could not be punished, the moral judgment of the world would be confused, and everyone led to the opinion that he had justified his godless doctrine.'[2]

Von Sickingen and Hutten tried to get Luther to join them, for they meditated open war. In those notes on Prierias, which mark his decisive break with Rome, Luther had indeed laid himself open to misrepresentation by quoting Psalm 58, 10: 'If we punish thieves with the gallows, robbers with the sword and heretics with fire, why do we not turn with force of arms against these teachers of iniquity . . . why do we not "wash our hands in their blood"?' Yet a few weeks later Luther made his

---

[1] P. Smith, *Luther's Correspondence*, p. 455.
[2] P. Smith, *Luther's Correspondence*, p. 419.

meaning plain when he described Hutten's anti-clerical plans as 'to make war on women and children'.[1] 'What Hutten is looking for, you see. I refuse to fight for the Gospel with force and slaughter. With the Word, the world was won, and by it the Church is preserved, and by it the Church will be restored. For as Antichrist arose without arms, so without arms will it be confounded.'[2] And in a phrase which he repeated in other letters: 'If the Gospel were of such a nature that it could be propagated or preserved by the powers of this world, God would not have entrusted it to fishermen.'[3] When the journey to Worms was determined, he wrote: 'If he [the Emperor] calls me to Worms in order to kill me, or because of my answer, to make me an enemy of the Empire, I shall offer to come. For I shall not run away (Christ helping me) nor shall I abandon the Word in this contest.'[4]

Not only Charles, but Frederick also, was uncertain whether it was wise to bring Luther to Worms. As the Diet drew near, the politicians liked the prospect less and less, and Glapion even persuaded Von Sickingen and Hutten that it would be better if Luther did not appear.[5] Even when the Imperial summons had gone out, the authorities hoped he would not obey. There was only one man to whom it had become increasingly simple and clear that he must go, and he was Martin Luther.

It was the climax of months of inner struggle. For Luther was no loud-mouthed fanatic with a hide like a rhinoceros. The taunts flung at him by his enemies found an echo in his own tormented self-questioning. 'How often has my trembling heart palpitated—are you alone the wise one? Are all the others in error? Have so many centuries walked in ignorance? What if it should be you who err, and drag so many with you into error, to be eternally damned?'[6] It was out of the darkness of such temptation (*Anfechtung*) that Luther found fortitude and calm, which shines out of his writings in these weeks, in the white heat of faith which the New Testament calls 'boldness' (*Parresia*), something we find reflected in the pages of the Acts of the

[1] WA Br.2.271.35.
[2] WA Br.2.249.13 (January 16th, 1521).
[3] WA Br.2.210.10 (November 4th, 1520).
[4] WA Br.2.289.11 (March 19th, 1521).
[5] K. Brandi, *Kaiser Karl V*, i, pp. 106 ff; ii, pp. 112 ff.
[6] WA 8.412.1; TR 1.51.4.

Apostles, in the Journals of John Wesley, and in not very many other places in Christian literature besides. There was no stopping him now. 'I shall enter Worms under my Captain, Christ, despite the gates of Hell,'[1] he told Philip, and 'I come, my Spalatin, and we shall enter Worms despite the gates of Hell, and the powers of the air.'[2] Months later he declared: 'When I came into Worms, had I known there were as many devils ready to spring upon me as there were tiles on the roofs, I would joyfully have sprung into the midst of them.'[3]

The Imperial Herald, Sturm, reached Wittenberg on March 26th. The politicians had outwitted Aleander who raged when he heard the name of the herald ('an impudent fool . . . clown . . . world-famous liar'). In fact, so far from being hushed up, the affair became a progress out of which the herald extracted full publicity value, as in village after village the people turned out to see, and sometimes to cheer. Luther himself was unwell, for great nervous strain always went to his stomach, if not to his heart. Two temptations to turn aside intervened with apocalyptic suddenness. News reached the party of an Imperial mandate against Luther's books, and the herald asked Luther if, in the circumstances, he would rather go back. 'I trembled,' said Luther, 'but said, "I'll go through with it".'[4] Finally (Satan disguised as an angel of light) Martin Bucer appeared to plead that Luther should take refuge with Hutten and Von Sickingen in the castle of the Ebernburg. He rode on.

On the morning of April 16th, a trumpet sounded and the crowd pressed towards the gates (Aleander's agent elbowing his way among them), as a proud cavalcade of nobles and knights clattered by; at the end the little covered wagon swaying round the bend. The crowd stared and murmured their fill at the Black monk who stared back with quick, shining eyes. At the Hospital of the Knights of St. John, Luther alighted, and 'looking about him with his demonic eyes, he exclaimed "God will be with me".'[5]

The next afternoon, he was escorted privately to the assembled Diet. He had to wait outside for two interminable hours, and

[1] WA Br.2.296.7 (April 7th). [2] WA Br.2.298.5 (April 14th).
[3] WA Br.2.455.52 (March 5th, 1522). [4] TR 3.282.8.
[5] P. Smith, *Luther's Correspondence*, p. 522.

then entered the crowded, tense assembly. It is no wonder that he turned nervously and a little jerkily from side to side, and greeted an old friend with excited and exaggerated cordiality. Before him, piled high, were the collected works of Martin Luther—so formidable that Charles V and Aleander refused to believe that one man, in a few months, could have composed them all. The official put the formal query whether Luther acknowledged the books to be his own, and Luther was about to reply, when the warning shout of his lawyer friend, Schurpf, rang out—'Let the titles be read!'

Luther turned, his body bent in the presence of Majesty, to confront the might of the Christian Empire, embodied in the pale, forbidding countenance of Charles, by God's Grace, Augmentor of the Realm of Germany; of Spain, the Two Sicilies, Jerusalem, Hungary, Dalmatia, Croatia, etc., King; Archduke of Austria, and Duke of Burgundy, etc., etc., and as the audience chamber focused on him in a moment of hushed silence, Luther's voice sounded faint and abashed. He did acknowledge his writings, he said, but since they involved faith, salvation and the Word of God, he asked time to consider. It was a good tactical move, though he disappointed the crowd. That evening he prepared a few notes (they have survived) which betray little agitation.

The next audience was in a more crowded and larger room. In the darkening hall, amid the smoking flares, Luther made his statement. He must discriminate between his writings: those of edification he could not retract; for too much violence in personal controversy he would gladly and humbly apologize; but about the reality of the Papal tyranny he must be adamant. He repeated his statement in Latin, and, the question being put whether he would recant, answered firmly: 'Unless I am proved wrong by the testimony of Scriptures or by evident reason [those who consider Luther the supreme irrationalist, should note!] I am bound in conscience and held fast to the Word of God . . . therefore I cannot and will not retract anything, for it is neither safe nor salutary to act against one's conscience. God help me. Amen.'[1]

It was not his greatest oration, lacking the famous apocryphal 'Here stand I. I can do no other. God help me. Amen'. Yet, as

[1] Boehmer, *Road to Reformation*, p. 415.

so often, a fine myth embodies the deeper truth. When we read J. A. Froude's comment, 'One of the finest—perhaps the finest scene in human history,'[1] the tendency to debunk is irresistible, for it could be suggested that Froude admired Luther for all the wrong reasons, that at this moment Luther had more in common with Hurrell, Froude and the men of the Oxford Movement than with the moralism of a liberal historian who cared little for theology but admired human heroism and the premonition of nineteenth-century liberty of thought. Not that the scene belies the great Protestant platitudes either, of liberty of conscience and obedience to the Word of God, though if this were the whole story we might have to find St. Thomas More a more perfect example of the former, and William Tyndale of the latter, since they resisted unto blood.

Nevertheless, had Luther succumbed to the enormous pressures put upon him to recant, whole ranges of European and Church history must have been different. Looking back, we realize the great forces on his side. When Kierkegaard reproached Luther for not having achieved martyrdom, it was hardly fair to Luther. That Luther did not suffer the fate of Huss was not due to lack of courageous witness or Luther's fault, but to the change in the climate of opinion after a century. But that this change was as great as it was, did not immediately appear. It has been said of the great strokes of the military art that they seem simple —afterwards! But place ourselves at the moment of uncertainty, weighed down with the possible consequences of inexorable decision—so it had been with Luther in these days when he accepted his revolutionary vocation with fear and trembling, amid a strain on body and nerve that left him a spent old man before his time. We can sympathize with Catholic historians who emphasize the appalling tragedy now enacted. Luther felt it to be appalling. Yet he made sure that if warfare had to come in Christendom, it should be the right war at the right place. But for him, the Reformation movement must have centred in those secondary issues which had preoccupied the Hussites and the later Lollards, and were to obsess the *Schwarmerei*, if, indeed, the whole matter of the Reformation had not been engulfed in a dark tide of greed and pride, or smothered among the fierce, secular energies of a new age.

[1] J. A. Froude, *Luther*, p. 33.

The Emperor cut short the audience with a quick, imperious gesture, and there was an ugly moment of confusion when some imagined Luther was put under arrest. But he reached safely the friendly faces, and as they pressed out into the hall Luther stretched out his arm like a victorious warrior, and his voice sounded clear above the din—'I am through! I am through!' The problem what to do next was a dilemma for Frederick as well as for the Emperor. They had demanded a hearing. Had not Luther been heard? Must he not come under the ban of the Empire? This was the view of the majority of the Electors, but the situation in the city was electric. In the night a placard was posted on the Town Hall of Worms, threatening violence on behalf of four hundred knights, and ending with the yet more alarming *Bundschuh! Bundschuh! Bundschuh!*—the peasant war cry which sent shivers down the not very firm spine of Albert of Mainz. Despite the speech of Charles V next day, affirming his own orthodoxy and repudiating Luther, the heretic was granted what he had asked vainly for three years, a hearing before learned and reasonably impartial judges. It was too late: in this topsy-turvy world, sentence had come first, then the judge's summing up, and now at long last the hearing. The debates were keen and courteous, but Luther had now committed his mind well beyond the limits even of the Conciliar theologians, and the discussions broke down, not over Papal authority, but on the subject of the fallibility of councils. They ended with Luther's final refusal: 'Even if I were to lose my body and my life on account of it, I cannot depart from the true Word of God.'

The latest Romanist apologist, Cochlaeus, impudently suggested that Luther might be prepared to surrender his safe-conduct for the pleasure of a debate with himself. This very silly suggestion nearly cost him his life, for on hearing it there were drawn swords among the German knights, who saw in it a transparent wile of Aleander (there they over-estimated his intelligence, not his morals). Amid a garbled and indignant report sent from Cochlaeus to Aleander there is one incident which may contain truth. Cochlaeus appealed to the witness of the Counts of Mansfeld 'whether they did not hear Luther say he would like the judge to be a boy of eight or nine years, or one of the pages whom he pointed out?'[1] Is it fanciful to think of

[1] P. Smith, *Luther's Correspondence*, p. 563.

Luther tousling the fair hair of a pageboy, and with august precedent setting him in the midst of the learned and noble, in anticipation of one of his own greatest sayings—'Thank God, a child of seven years old knows what the Church is, namely, the Holy believers and the Lambs who hear the Shepherd's Voice.'?

Throughout, Luther had shown a simplicity which is a mark of greatness. Had he been a man of guile, or even had he consented to play the politician, or even to be guided by the politicians, the Wars of Religion might have begun in the streets of Worms in April, 1521. We should treat seriously Luther's later statement:

'I simply taught, preached, wrote God's Word: otherwise I did nothing. And then, while I slept, or drank Wittenberg beer with my Philip and my Amsdorf, the Word so greatly weakened the Papacy that never a Prince or Emperor inflicted such damage upon it. I did nothing. The Word did it all. Had I desired to foment trouble, I could have brought great bloodshed upon Germany. Yea, I could have started such a little game at Worms, that the Emperor would not have been safe. But what would it have been? A mug's game. I left it to the Word.'[1] The Imperial Ban would follow (it was not signed until May 26th, with the assent of a rump Diet, and the edict was no theological masterpiece). Meanwhile Luther had departed, and bidding farewell to the escorting knights and the Imperial Herald, he moved slowly homeward towards Wittenberg on a journey which, for a public enemy, seemed likely to be calm and uneventful.

If any justification were needed for calling Luther by Kierkegaard's fine phrase, 'the Knight of Faith', it is to be found in the remarkable book the writing of which was actually interrupted by the journey to Worms. There were not many who, in such circumstances, could have concentrated upon an exposition of the *Magnificat*. Luther wrote it for the young Prince, John Frederick of Saxony, and it contains material for a philosophy of the place of power in history. There are passages of almost womanish tenderness (a side of Luther's character not to be confused with Teutonic sentimentalism) and beauty. 'She does not proclaim with a loud voice that she is the Mother of God— but goes about her wonted household duties, milking the cows,

[1] WML 2.399 (1522).

cooking the meals, washing pots and kettles, sweeping out the rooms, and performing the work of maidservant or housewife in lowly and despised tasks as though she cared nothing for such exceeding great gifts and graces.'[1] That loving insight into nature which Heinrich Bornkamm suggests to be a side of Luther which later Protestantism neglected to its cost, appears here, as Luther considers the ingratitude of man: 'If they looked beneath them, they would find many that have not half of what they have and yet are content in God, and sing His praises. A bird pipes his song and is happy in its gifts: nor does it murmur because it has not the gift of speech; a dog frisks gaily about and is content . . . all animals live in contentment and serve God loving and praising Him. Only the grudging, evil eye of man is never satisfied.'[2]

Most striking of all, the tract contains material for a philosophy of history, a profound diagnosis of the might and vulnerability of human pride, that 'bubble'-like quality by which arrogance resting on violence has been able, again and again, to stretch and swell into vast and terrifying systems of empire, battening upon great historical forces, until it seems to be invincible, until, with breathtaking suddenness, its hour comes (what Luther called a *stundlein*, and the Bible *kairos*) when God stretches forth His finger and the vast balloon collapses, and the once paralysing and terrifying painted face upon it sags into sudden ruin, like Egypt, Babylon, the Third Reich.

'God lets them puff themselves up in their own power alone. For where man's strength begins, God's strength ends. When their bubble is full blown, and everyone supposes them to have won and overcome, and they feel themselves safe and secure, then God pricks the bubble—and it is all over . . . therefore their prosperity has its day, disappears like a bubble, and is as if it had never been.'[3] 'For God does not destroy the mighty as suddenly as they deserve, but lets them go for a season until their might has reached its highest point. When it has done this, God does not support it, neither can it support itself: it breaks

[1] WML 3.164.
[2] WML 3.153. H. Bornkamm, *Luther's Geistige Welt* (*Das Bild der Natur*), pp. 172 ff.
[3] WML 3.179.

down of its own weight without any crash or sound . . . for while the earth remains, authority, rule, power . . . must needs remain. But God will not suffer men to abuse them. He puts down one kingdom and exalts another; increases one people and destroys another: as He did with Assyria, Babylon, Persia, Greece and Rome, though they thought they should sit in their seats for ever.'[1]

The critical date of these utterances suggests a striking hypothesis. In the Latin, the word for 'bubble' (*bulla*) is the same as the word used for a Papal Bull, and in other writings Luther often puns upon the double meaning. One is bound to ask whether Luther's profound meditation on the character of earthly tyranny was not evoked by the fact of the Papal Bull, that symbol of what he had come to see as a great earthly tyranny resting upon pride and violence? It explains a good deal, if it is so. For Luther saw a deep truth. In fact Ecclesiastical Man, no less than Political and Economic Man, has to reckon with power, is tempted by it, and had come in the Middle Ages to build up a mighty system which had seemed to men to be invincible, but which the events of 1521 had shown to have decayed within, and to be more vulnerable than any had dreamed. For Luther the Papacy could not merely be a system of earthly sovereignty like other empires: it was the degradation of spiritual power, and so invited a more dreadful judgment than any earthly tyranny. We can see how Luther came to see the Papacy as Antichrist, even though Luther himself did not see all the truth. But we have to set over and against this the triumphant confidence of Luther's comfort to the meek and oppressed in this exposition of 'the *Marseillaise* of all poor devils.' 'We too shall see the mercy of God together with all His might . . . we suppose our cause to have lost and our enemies to have won . . . because we do not know His proper works, and therefore do not know Him, neither His mercy, nor His arm. For He must and will be known by Faith.'[2] So once again it is faith which gives unity to the writing—'Such a faith has life and being: it pervades and changes the whole man—to this faith all things are possible.'[3]

Luther reached Eisenach, and preached there on May 3rd. Then he visited his kinsmen at Möhra. As they rode away

[1] WML 3.183.   [2] WML 3.179.   [3] WML 3.136.

through the woods, a band of horsemen swept round them, throwing the little party into confusion and flight, but carrying off Luther, clinging to his books, into the darkening forest glades; nor did they pause until, late that night, the dark shadow of the Wartburg loomed black against the stars. They rattled over the drawbridge, into the lights and bustle of the castle yard. The great moment was over. Luther had proved the power of faith to overcome the world. There remained the flesh—and the Devil.

EPILOGUE

THE OLDER HISTORIANS were not wrong in singling out the Diet of Worms as marking a landmark in the story of the Reformation, though it is of the order of events which reveal, rather than inaugurate, historical forces. We have seen that the theological development of Luther is an integral part of its context. To trace that development in detail (beginning with Luther's marginal notes of 1509 and finding a halting place in his fine *Contra Latomus* (1521)) demands skill and care. It is not immediately evident, since Luther uses scholastic jargon and Augustinian categories long after the direction of his thought has changed. The full extent of continuity and discontinuity in Luther's thought will not be clarified until studies of late scholasticism are further advanced.

May we speak, after the *motif* research[1] of the Scandinavians, of a coherent centre of Luther's theology, or is it, as Lortz supposes, a tumultuous, genial, inchoate flood? May we speak with the Swedish theologian, Anders Nygren, of Luther's *Copernican Revolution*, his substitution of a God-centred doctrine of redemption for the man-centred theology of the late Middle Ages?[2] Or, with the Danish theologian, Regin Prenter, of Luther's return to the biblical realism, of personal encounter with God, in contrast to the mediæval and Augustinian doctrines of 'infused charity'?[3] Or, with the Finnish scholar, Lennart Pinomaa, of the break-through of Luther from formal and academic notions to a genuinely 'existential' theology relating thought and life?[4] To this last, the Catholic Lortz makes large and unconscious concessions when he recognizes the failure of even Thomism, in sixteenth-century Germany, to do more than provide a cold and 'correct' intellectual answer to the poignant questions raised by Luther.

[1] E. M. Carlson, *The Re-interpretation of Luther*, Philadelphia 1948, pp. 36–44.
[2] A. Nygren, *Eros and Agape*, Pt. II, vol. i, 1938, pp. 463 ff; P. S. Watson, *Let God be God*, 1947, pp. 33 ff.
[3] R. Prenter, *Spiritus Creator*, Copenhagen 1946, pp. 80 ff.
[4] L. Pinomaa, *Der Existentielle Charakter der Theologie Luthers*, Helsinki 1940.

Positively these fine expositions are based on deep research. How far, negatively, and with one deadly phrase, mediæval theology can be written off, is another question. The expositions of MM. Gilson and P. Vignaux would seem to demand a re-examination of that side of the question. Luther, says J. Lortz, 'constructed a new world'.[1] He carried through a drastic simplification of late mediæval theology, rejecting its philosophic envelope, and returning to 'the Bible and the old Fathers'.[2]

The word 'restatement' has been so grossly abused that it is probably unwise to use it, but something like it does occur when new categories of thought with new relations to one another, and with a new technical vocabulary, are erected (in Luther's case, on the fundament of the Bible). The controversy between Catholic and Protestant is more than the Great Misunderstanding, but since the ecumenical conversations ceased (about 1541) there has been a persistent element of genuine misunderstanding, due to the insistence of both orthodoxies in interpreting the other's words in terms of their own defined meaning.

But when allowance has been made for criticism of him, and when it is recognized that an infallible Luther is no part of any Protestant confession, when it is allowed that much of Protestant life and thought has another origin than in Luther, the Protestant churches have mainly persisted throughout four centuries upon the theological foundation of justification by faith, Luther's assessment of the biblical gospel, in a way inconceivable had it been the mere concatenation of errors of older Catholic description, or the hodge-podge of incoherences and subjectivism of recent Catholic comment. Chesterton's great saying that Newman, apart from his Catholicism, would not have been Newman, but something quite different, must be applied to Luther and his influence (the old assertion that all that is good in Luther is Catholic, is a naïve begging of the question). The music of J. S. Bach, the hymns of Paul Gerhardt, the philanthropy of Francke, the passion with which Heinrich Wichern launched the great 'Innere Mission', the witness of Dietrich Bonhoeffer, Martin Niemöller and Eivvind Berggrav

---

[1] J. Lortz, *Die Reformation in Deutschland*, 1.201.
[2] Luther's appeal to history and tradition was far more earnest than the rhetorical flourish Newman supposed it to be.

are rich diversities of Christian character and expression which owe something characteristic to Luther's teaching. They provide a *prima facie* case for the sympathetic reconsideration of his theology.

We have halted on the verge of Luther's creative achievement. Those grievously err who see a merely negative and destructive meaning in the Protestant Reformation. Who in 1510 could have imagined that within a generation there would exist new forms of Christian language and worship, clothed in new forms of Christian institutions and discipline, new pieties, capable of growth, of transmutation and development, of nourishing innumerable holy souls? Consider Luther's literary work: the vast correspondence in that neat, small, scholarly hand, which overflows many folio volumes, and dealt with practical and spiritual problems across half Europe, and for half a century. And the serried ranks, volume upon volume, of his other writings testify to the prodigious energy which could produce something like a writing a fortnight over twenty-five years. Much of it is second-rate and of ephemeral value, but much also of imperishable worth. He was a fine pamphleteer and wrote scores of pamphlets, every one of them what Humpty Dumpty would call 'a nice, knock-down argument for you'. And he wrote from his heart, and out it came, tumbling hot and choking with anger, or shaking with laughter, but always lucid, always able to be understanded of the people.

For the rest, compare the list of those who in England must do a work comparable with his. He gave his people their open Bible, was to them what Tyndale, Coverdale and Rogers were to us; if anything, his German Bible was more important. He could shape a liturgy as well as Thomas Cranmer, though he did not fall into our error of abolishing that variety on which the continuing life of liturgy depends. Luther wrote a classical catechism which has really no parallel in English (for even the Shorter Catechism hardly survives its magnificent opening lines). He was as great a preacher as Hugh Latimer, and his sermons had effect comparable with the Book of Homilies. For a collection of hymns like his, England had to wait until Isaac Watts. His commentaries and theological works have never been fully explored, let alone exhausted. We remember how John Bunyan got hold of Luther's *Galatians* and said, 'I found my condition in his experience so largely and profoundly handled as if the book had been written out of my heart', and how the reading of Luther's preface to the Romans was the occasion of the evangelical conversion of John Wesley. Luther did in twenty years almost single-handed what it took six notable Englishmen the span of two centuries to accomplish: beside that which came upon him daily, the care of the churches, the fighting against Popery and the fanatics, the forming a communion world wide and recognizably his debtor. This is to say nothing of his great services to education, and church music, and a dozen other weighty matters.

The man counts, too. To our six Englishmen we might add a seventh. In the Strand, in London, stands a figure, burly and blunt, reading from a book. It might almost—*mutatis mutandis*—be Luther, but it is Samuel Johnson. The two men had much of their greatness in common, in their plain common sense, their humour and their melancholy, their delight at shocking their friends, the pathos of their inner struggles, and the loyalty and love they contrived to keep among their friends. Perhaps Luther was less fortunate in the dozen or so inferior Boswells who were permitted to frequent his table and whose garbled and sometimes fuddled remembrances, recorded in the *Table Talk*, are not always faithful and true. But at least we can see Luther and Johnson at home. Nobody ever wore his heart more on his sleeve than Luther, and there for all to see are his fun and tenderness, his deep love of his family and his home, his mighty prayers, and the vulgarity which prevents us thinking of him as some stained-glass figure, or cloying his memory with sickly romanticism. For there are shadows as well as lights.

Luther lived to see the Reformation become a great movement, under the most diverse leadership. It can be confessed that there is more to be said for Karlstadt, Münzer and the Peasants, for Zwingli and the Zwinglians, than Luther ever saw or believed. He lived on the edge of time, and believed that the Papacy was just another human institution swollen in arrogance and power, and now toppling to its doom, the engine of Antichrist. This was worse than a crime: it was a mistake. That Luther could be brutal and violent, that the physical impact of a dozen ailments affected his temper and his manners, cannot be gainsaid. But he had great virtues too, including the two indispensable characteristics of moral greatness, simplicity and magnanimity.

We cannot even broach the subject of the influence of Luther upon the subsequent course of German history. The studies of Törnvall and Wingren[1] in recent years have shown how profound and subtle is Luther's teaching of the two realms of spiritual and temporal authority, how remote from the ethical dualism of modern German political development. On the whole, perhaps the chief villain of German history is—History: the vast complexity of social, economic, political pressures, the long entail of the past as it touches the future. Decisive differences appear when we compare the German and English political scene on the verge of the Reformation, and the Thirty Years' War was to influence and deepen them far more radically than any misunderstanding and misappropriation of the meaning of Luther.

Now, Luther has more to tell us than almost any of the sixteenth-century Reformers. His doctrine of Justification by Faith, his conception of history, recover that eschatological context which modern biblical theology is interpreting anew. The revival of Continental theology associated with Karl Barth has behind it the 'Luther renaissance' of the last thirty years. Luther himself did not take kindly to the idea that men might at some distant date study his writings, when they would be better employed studying the Word of God. Now, Protestants must be occupied with nothing less than the Reformation of Reformation itself. The characteristic language, forms, institutions, disciplines, which began four hundred years ago, have come to the end of their journey, as evangelical and pastoral vehicles, however imperishable their value to the trained and instructed within the household of faith. If our gospel is to come home to lost, secular, revolutionary man, the Churches of East and West, Catholic and Protestant, must face the need for creative and drastic change. Within our lifetime new forms of Christian existence may need to arise as different from those of the past, as the world of modern Protestantism differs from that of the later Middle Ages. Here Luther would encourage us. 'For what, I ask,' he said, 'is not new that faith does? Was it not a new

---

[1] G. Törnvall, *Andligt och världsligt regemente hos Luther*, Stockholm 1940; G. Wingren, *Luthers Lara om Kallelsen*, Lund 1948.

thing when the Apostles instituted their ministry? Was it not a new thing, when Abraham offered his son? Was it not new when Israel crossed the sea? Will it not be a new thing when I shall pass from death to life?' Luther bids us look beyond Ecclesiastical Man, even in the guise of prophet and Reformer, to the inspiring prospect of history as the royal progress of the Word of God, going forth conquering and to conquer.

INDEX

ALBERT, PRINCE OF BRANDENBURG, 51

Aleander, 80, 92, 93, 95, 96, 98

Aquinas, St. Thomas, 12, 17

Aristotle, 12, 17, 19, 20, 22, 40, 46, 90

Augustine, St., 19, 21, 22, 26, 34, 39, 40, 42, 77, 81

BAPTISM, Sacrament of, 82, 85, 86

Biel, Gabriel, 17, 19, 28, 46, 50

CAJETAN, CARDINAL, 58, 60–62, 77, 80

Cochlaeus, 71, 98

ECK, DR. JOHN, 64–71, 80, 85, 92

Erasmus, 18, 22, 76–79

FAITH, 33, 41, 44, 47, 53, 56, 73–76, 86, 88, 89, 96, 101, 102, 104, 107

Frederick the Wise, Elector of Saxony, 19, 52, 60, 62–64, 79, 94, 98

GOSPEL, 39, 56

Grace, Doctrine of, 22, 35

HUMANISTS, 76–78, 84

Huss, John, 69, 97

Hutten, Ulrich von, 76, 79, 80, 92–95

INDULGENCE, 50–53, 55, 56, 59, 69

JONAS, JUSTUS, 13

Justice of God, 33, 34, 38

Justification, 22, 35, 41, 53, 72, 73, 85, 104, 107

KARLSTADT, ANDREAS, 45, 65–69, 106

LANG, JOHN, 23, 43, 45, 46, 56

Leipzig, Disputation at, 67, 70

Liberty of a Christian Man, 81, 86

Lombard, Peter, 19, 21, 22, 39, 41

Lortz, J., 16, 39, 51, 64, 69, 103, 104

MANSFELD, 9–11

Melanchthon, 13, 15, 63, 67, 77, 78, 95, 99

Miltitz, Chas. von, 62, 64, 65, 68, 72, 80

Mystics, 42, 43

NOMINALISTS, 12, 17–19, 31, 34, 45–47, 56

OCCAM, WM. OF, 12, 17–19, 46

PENANCE, Sacrament of, 51, 85

Predestination, Doctrine of, 32, 42, 43

Prierias, 64, 71, 93

Priesthood of All Believers, 83, 86, 88

Psalms, 36–38

RESIGNATION, Doctrine of, 43

SANCTIFICATION, 41

Scotus, 17–19, 46, 57

Sickingen von, 80, 93–95

Staupitz, Johannes von, 15, 20, 22–24, 26, 31, 32, 42, 54–57, 60, 61, 81

TAULER, 43

Temptation, Doctrine of, 73

Tetzel, John, 52, 55, 57, 64, 65, 68

Theology of the Cross, 47, 56

Transubstantiation, Doctrine of, 85

WORD of God, 39, 54, 85–87, 94, 96–99, 107, 108

Worms, Diet of, 93–95, 99, 103

Wrath of God, 29, 30, 44, 47–49, 53, 71, 82, 84, 86

ZWINGLI, 18, 77, 78, 106

Revised August, 1964

hARPER ✦ tORChBOOKS

HUMANITIES AND SOCIAL SCIENCES

American Studies

JOHN R. ALDEN: The American Revolution, 1775-1783.† *Illus.*   TB/3011

RAY STANNARD BAKER: Following the Color Line: *American Negro Citizenship in the Progressive Era.‡ Illus. Edited by Dewey W. Grantham, Jr.*   TB/3053

RAY A. BILLINGTON: The Far Western Frontier, 1830-1860.† *Illus.*   TB/3012

JOSEPH L. BLAU, Ed.: Cornerstones of Religious Freedom in America. *Selected Basic Documents, Court Decisions and Public Statements. Enlarged and revised edition with new Intro. by Editor*   TB/118

RANDOLPH S. BOURNE: War and the Intellectuals: *Collected Essays, 1915-1919.‡ Edited by Carl Resek*   TB/3043

A. RUSSELL BUCHANAN: The United States and World War II. † *Illus.*   Volume I TB/3044
                                   Volume II TB/3045

ABRAHAM CAHAN: The Rise of David Levinsky: *a novel. Introduction by John Higham*   TB/1028

JOSEPH CHARLES: The Origins of the American Party System   TB/1049

THOMAS C. COCHRAN: The Inner Revolution: *Essays on the Social Sciences in History*   TB/1140

T. C. COCHRAN & WILLIAM MILLER: The Age of Enterprise: *A Social History of Industrial America*   TB/1054

EDWARD S. CORWIN: American Constitutional History: *Essays edited by Alpheus T. Mason and Gerald Garvey*   TB/1136

FOSTER RHEA DULLES: America's Rise to World Power, 1898-1954.† *Illus.*   TB/3021

W. A. DUNNING: Reconstruction, Political and Economic, 1865-1877   TB/1073

A. HUNTER DUPREE: Science in the Federal Government: *A History of Policies and Activities to 1940*   TB/573

CLEMENT EATON: The Growth of Southern Civilization, 1790-1860.† *Illus.*   TB/3040

HAROLD U. FAULKNER: Politics, Reform and Expansion, 1890-1900.† *Illus.*   TB/3020

LOUIS FILLER: The Crusade against Slavery, 1830-1860.† *Illus.*   TB/3029

EDITORS OF FORTUNE: America in the Sixties: *the Economy and the Society. Two-color charts* TB/1015

LAWRENCE HENRY GIPSON: The Coming of the Revolution, 1763-1775.† *Illus.*   TB/3007

FRANCIS J. GRUND: Aristocracy in America: *Jacksonian Democracy*   TB/1001

ALEXANDER HAMILTON: The Reports of Alexander Hamilton.‡ *Edited by Jacob E. Cooke*   TB/3060

OSCAR HANDLIN, Editor: This Was America: *As Recorded by European Travelers to the Western Shore in the Eighteenth, Nineteenth, and Twentieth Centuries. Illus.*   TB/1119

MARCUS LEE HANSEN: The Atlantic Migration: 1607-1860. *Edited by Arthur M. Schlesinger; Introduction by Oscar Handlin*   TB/1052

MARCUS LEE HANSEN: The Immigrant in American History. *Edited with a Foreword by Arthur Schlesinger, Sr.*   TB/1120

JOHN D. HICKS: Republican Ascendancy, 1921-1933.† *Illus.*   TB/3041

JOHN HIGHAM, Ed.: The Reconstruction of American History   TB/1068

DANIEL R. HUNDLEY: Social Relations in our Southern States.‡ *Edited by William R. Taylor*   TB/3058

ROBERT H. JACKSON: The Supreme Court in the American System of Government   TB/1106

THOMAS JEFFERSON: Notes on the State of Virginia.‡ *Edited by Thomas Perkins Abernethy*   TB/3052

WILLIAM L. LANGER & S. EVERETT GLEASON: The Challenge to Isolation: *The World Crisis of 1937-1940 and American Foreign Policy*   Volume I TB/3054
                                   Volume II TB/3055

WILLIAM E. LEUCHTENBURG: Franklin D. Roosevelt and the New Deal, 1932-1940.† *Illus.*   TB/3025

LEONARD W. LEVY: Freedom of Speech and Press in Early American History: *Legacy of Suppression*   TB/1109

ARTHUR S. LINK: Woodrow Wilson and the Progressive Era, 1910-1917.† *Illus.*   TB/3023

ROBERT GREEN McCLOSKEY: American Conservatism in the Age of Enterprise, 1865-1910   TB/1137

BERNARD MAYO: Myths and Men: *Patrick Henry, George Washington, Thomas Jefferson*   TB/1108

JOHN C. MILLER: Alexander Hamilton and the Growth of the New Nation   TB/3057

JOHN C. MILLER: The Federalist Era, 1789-1801.† *Illus.*   TB/3027

---

† The New American Nation Series, edited by Henry Steele Commager and Richard B. Morris.

‡ American Perspectives series, edited by Bernard Wishy and William E. Leuchtenburg.

* The Rise of Modern Europe series, edited by William L. Langer.

❙ Researches in the Social, Cultural, and Behavioral Sciences, edited by Benjamin Nelson.

§ The Library of Religion and Culture, edited by Benjamin Nelson.

Σ Harper Modern Science Series, edited by James R. Newman.

◦ Not for sale in Canada.

PERRY MILLER: Errand into the Wilderness TB/1139
PERRY MILLER & T. H. JOHNSON, Editors: The Puritans: *A Sourcebook of Their Writings*
Volume I TB/1093
Volume II TB/1094
GEORGE E. MOWRY: The Era of Theodore Roosevelt and the Birth of Modern America, 1900-1912.† *Illus.*
TB/3022
WALLACE NOTESTEIN: The English People on the Eve of Colonization, 1603-1630.† *Illus.* TB/3006
RUSSEL BLAINE NYE: The Cultural Life of the New Nation, 1776-1801.† *Illus.* TB/3026
RALPH BARTON PERRY: Puritanism and Democracy
TB/1138
GEORGE E. PROBST, Ed.: The Happy Republic: *A Reader in Tocqueville's America* TB/1060
WALTER RAUSCHENBUSCH: Christianity and the Social Crisis.‡ *Edited by Robert D. Cross* TB/3059
FRANK THISTLETHWAITE: America and the Atlantic Community: *Anglo-American Aspects, 1790-1850*
TB/1107
TWELVE SOUTHERNERS: I'll Take My Stand: *The South and the Agrarian Tradition. Introduction by Louis D. Rubin, Jr.; Biographical Essays by Virginia Rock* TB/1072
A. F. TYLER: Freedom's Ferment: *Phases of American Social History from the Revolution to the Outbreak of the Civil War. Illus.* TB/1074
GLYNDON G. VAN DEUSEN: The Jacksonian Era, 1828-1848.† *Illus.* TB/3028
WALTER E. WEYL: The New Democracy: *An Essay on Certain Political and Economic Tendencies in the United States.‡ Edited by Charles Forcey* TB/3042
LOUIS B. WRIGHT: The Cultural Life of the American Colonies, 1607-1763.† *Illus.* TB/3005
LOUIS B. WRIGHT: Culture on the Moving Frontier
TB/1053

Anthropology & Sociology

BERNARD BERELSON, Ed.: The Behavioral Sciences Today TB/1127
JOSEPH B. CASAGRANDE, Ed.: In the Company of Man: *20 Portraits of Anthropological Informants. Illus.* TB/3047
W. E. LE GROS CLARK: The Antecedents of Man: *An Introduction to the Evolution of the Primates.º Illus.*
TB/559
THOMAS C. COCHRAN: The Inner Revolution: *Essays on the Social Sciences in History*
TB/1140
ALLISON DAVIS & JOHN DOLLARD: Children of Bondage: *The Personality Development of Negro Youth in the Urban South*‖ TB/3049
ST. CLAIR DRAKE & HORACE R. CAYTON: Black Metropolis: *A Study of Negro Life in a Northern City. Introduction by Everett C. Hughes. Tables, maps, charts and graphs* Volume I TB/1086
Volume II TB/1087
CORA DU BOIS: The People of Alor. *New Preface by the author. Illus.* Volume I TB/1042
Volume II TB/1043
LEON FESTINGER, HENRY W. RIECKEN & STANLEY SCHACHTER: When Prophecy Fails: *A Social and Psychological Account of a Modern Group that Predicted the Destruction of the World*‖ TB/1132
RAYMOND FIRTH, Ed.: Man and Culture: *An Evaluation of the Work of Bronislaw Malinowski*‖º
TB/1133

L. S. B. LEAKEY: Adam's Ancestors: *The Evolution of Man and his Culture. Illus.* TB/1019
KURT LEWIN: Field Theory in Social Science: *Selected Theoretical Papers.*‖ *Edited with a Foreword by Dorwin Cartwright* TB/1135
ROBERT H. LOWIE: Primitive Society. *Introduction by Fred Eggan* TB/1056
BENJAMIN NELSON: Religious Traditions and the Spirit of Capitalism: *From the Church Fathers to Jeremy Bentham* TB/1130
TALCOTT PARSONS & EDWARD A. SHILS, Editors: Toward a General Theory of Action: *Theoretical Foundations for the Social Sciences* TB/1083
JOHN H. ROHRER & MUNRO S. EDMONSON, Eds.: The Eighth Generation Grows Up: *Cultures and Personalities of New Orleans Negroes*‖ TB/3050
ARNOLD ROSE: The Negro in America: *The Condensed Version of Gunnar Myrdal's An American Dilemma. New Introduction by the Author; Foreword by Gunnar Myrdal* TB/3048
KURT SAMUELSSON: Religion and Economic Action: *A Critique of Max Weber's The Protestant Ethic and the Spirit of Capitalism.*‖º *Trans. by E. G. French; Ed. with Intro. by D. C. Coleman* TB/1131
PITIRIM SOROKIN: Contemporary Sociological Theories: *Through the First Quarter of the Twentieth Century* TB/3046
MAURICE R. STEIN: The Eclipse of Community: *An Interpretation of American Studies. New Introduction by the Author* TB/1128
SIR EDWARD TYLOR: The Origins of Culture. *Part I of "Primitive Culture."§ Introduction by Paul Radin*
TB/33
SIR EDWARD TYLOR: Religion in Primitive Culture. *Part II of "Primitive Culture."§ Introduction by Paul Radin* TB/34
W. LLOYD WARNER & Associates: Democracy in Jonesville: *A Study in Quality and Inequality**
TB/1129
W. LLOYD WARNER: A Black Civilization: *A Study of an Australian Tribe.*‖ *Illus.* TB/3056
W. LLOYD WARNER: Social Class in America: *The Evaluation of Status* TB/1013

Art and Art History

EMILE MÂLE: The Gothic Image: *Religious Art in France of the Thirteenth Century.§ 190 illus.* TB/44
MILLARD MEISS: Painting in Florence and Siena after the Black Death. *169 illus.* TB/1148
ERWIN PANOFSKY: Studies in Iconology: *Humanistic Themes in the Art of the Renaissance. 180 illustrations* TB/1077
ALEXANDRE PIANKOFF: The Shrines of Tut-Ankh-Amon. *Edited by N. Rambova. 117 illus.* TB/2011
JEAN SEZNEC: The Survival of the Pagan Gods: *The Mythological Tradition and Its Place in Renaissance Humanism and Art. 108 illustrations* TB/2004
OTTO VON SIMSON: The Gothic Cathedral: *Origins of Gothic Architecture and the Medieval Concept of Order. 58 illus.* TB/2018
HEINRICH ZIMMER: Myths and Symbols in Indian Art and Civilization. *70 illustrations* TB/2005

Business, Economics & Economic History

REINHARD BENDIX: Work and Authority in Industry: *Ideologies of Management in the Course of Industrialization* TB/3035

2

THOMAS C. COCHRAN: The American Business System: *A Historical Perspective, 1900-1955*   TB/1080
ROBERT DAHL & CHARLES E. LINDBLOM: Politics, Economics, and Welfare: *Planning and Politico-Economic Systems Resolved into Basic Social Processes*   TB/3037
PETER F. DRUCKER: The New Society: *The Anatomy of Industrial Order*   TB/1082
ROBERT L. HEILBRONER: The Great Ascent: *The Struggle for Economic Development in Our Time*   TB/3030
ABBA P. LERNER: Everybody's Business: *A Re-examination of Current Assumptions in Economics and Public Policy*   TB/3051
ROBERT GREEN McCLOSKEY: American Conservatism in the Age of Enterprise, 1865-1910   TB/1137
PAUL MANTOUX: The Industrial Revolution in the Eighteenth Century: *The Beginnings of the Modern Factory System in England*⁰   TB/1079
WILLIAM MILLER, Ed.: Men in Business: *Essays on the Historical Role of the Entrepreneur*   TB/1081
PERRIN STRYKER: The Character of the Executive: *Eleven Studies in Managerial Qualities*   TB/1041
PIERRE URI: Partnership for Progress: *A Program for Transatlantic Action*   TB/3036

Contemporary Culture

JACQUES BARZUN: The House of Intellect   TB/1051
JOHN U. NEF: Cultural Foundations of Industrial Civilization   TB/1024
PAUL VALÉRY: The Outlook for Intelligence   TB/2016

History: General

L. CARRINGTON GOODRICH: A Short History of the Chinese People. *Illus.*   TB/3015
BERNARD LEWIS: The Arabs in History   TB/1029
SIR PERCY SYKES: A History of Exploration.⁰ *Introduction by John K. Wright*   TB/1046

History: Ancient and Medieval

A. ANDREWES: The Greek Tyrants   TB/1103
P. BOISSONNADE: Life and Work in Medieval Europe.⁰ *Preface by Lynn White, Jr.*   TB/1141
HELEN CAM: England before Elizabeth   TB/1026
NORMAN COHN: The Pursuit of the Millennium: *Revolutionary Messianism in medieval and Reformation Europe and its bearing on modern Leftist and Rightist totalitarian movements*   TB/1037
G. G. COULTON: Medieval Village, Manor, and Monastery   TB/1022
HEINRICH FICHTENAU: The Carolingian Empire: *The Age of Charlemagne*   TB/1142
F. L. GANSHOF: Feudalism   TB/1058
J. M. HUSSEY: The Byzantine World   TB/1057
SAMUEL NOAH KRAMER: Sumerian Mythology   TB/1055
FERDINAND LOT: The End of the Ancient World and the Beginnings of the Middle Ages. *Introduction by Glanville Downey*   TB/1044
STEVEN RUNCIMAN: A History of the Crusades. Volume I: *The First Crusade and the Foundation of the Kingdom of Jerusalem. Illus.*   TB/1143

HENRY OSBORN TAYLOR: The Classical Heritage of the Middle Ages. *Foreword and Biblio. by Kenneth M. Setton* [Formerly listed as TB/48 under the title *The Emergence of Christian Culture in the West*]   TB/1117
J. M. WALLACE-HADRILL: The Barbarian West: *The Early Middle Ages, A.D. 400-1000*   TB/1061

History: Renaissance & Reformation

R. R. BOLGAR: The Classical Heritage and Its Beneficiaries: *From the Carolingian Age to the End of the Renaissance*   TB/1125
JACOB BURCKHARDT: The Civilization of the Renaissance in Italy. *Introduction by Benjamin Nelson and Charles Trinkaus. Illus.*   Volume I TB/40
   Volume II TB/41
ERNST CASSIRER: The Individual and the Cosmos in Renaissance Philosophy. *Translated with an Introduction by Mario Domandi*   TB/1097
EDWARD P. CHEYNEY: The Dawn of a New Era, 1250-1453.* *Illus.*   TB/3002
WALLACE K. FERGUSON, et al.: Facets of the Renaissance   TB/1098
WALLACE K. FERGUSON, et al.: The Renaissance: *Six Essays. Illus.*   TB/1084
MYRON P. GILMORE: The World of Humanism, 1453-1517.* *Illus.*   TB/3003
JOHAN HUIZINGA: Erasmus and the Age of Reformation. *Illus.*   TB/19
ULRICH VON HUTTEN, et al.: On the Eve of the Reformation: *"Letters of Obscure Men." Introduction by Hajo Holborn*   TB/1124
PAUL O. KRISTELLER: Renaissance Thought: *The Classic, Scholastic, and Humanist Strains*   TB/1048
NICCOLÒ MACHIAVELLI: History of Florence and of the Affairs of Italy: *from the earliest times to the death of Lorenzo the Magnificent. Introduction by Felix Gilbert*   TB/1027
ALFRED VON MARTIN: Sociology of the Renaissance. *Introduction by Wallace K. Ferguson*   TB/1099
MILLARD MEISS: Painting in Florence and Siena after the Black Death. *169 illus.*   TB/1148
J. E. NEALE: The Age of Catherine de Medici⁰   TB/1085
ERWIN PANOFSKY: Studies in Iconology: *Humanistic Themes in the Art of the Renaissance. 180 illustrations*   TB/1077
J. H. PARRY: The Establishment of the European Hegemony: 1415-1715: *Trade and Exploration in the Age of the Renaissance*   TB/1045
HENRI PIRENNE: Early Democracies in the Low Countries: *Urban Society and Political Conflict in the Middle Ages and the Renaissance. Introduction by John Mundy*   TB/1110
FERDINAND SCHEVILL: The Medici. *Illus.*   TB/1010
FERDINAND SCHEVILL: Medieval and Renaissance Florence. *Illus.* Volume I: *Medieval Florence* TB/1090
   Volume II: *The Coming of Humanism and the Age of the Medici*   TB/1091
G. M. TREVELYAN: England in the Age of Wycliffe, 1368-1520⁰   TB/1112
VESPASIANO: Renaissance Princes, Popes, and Prelates: *The Vespasiano Memoirs: Lives of Illustrious Men of the XVth Century. Introduction by Myron P. Gilmore*   TB/1111

3

History: Modern European

FREDERICK B. ARTZ: Reaction and Revolution, 1815-1832.* *Illus.*   TB/3034
MAX BELOFF: The Age of Absolutism, 1660-1815
                                                   TB/1062
ROBERT C. BINKLEY: Realism and Nationalism, 1852-1871.* *Illus.*   TB/3038
CRANE BRINTON: A Decade of Revolution, 1789-1799.* *Illus.*   TB/3018
J. BRONOWSKI & BRUCE MAZLISH: The Western Intellectual Tradition: *From Leonardo to Hegel*
                                                   TB/3001
GEOFFREY BRUUN: Europe and the French Imperium, 1799-1814.* *Illus.*   TB/3033
ALAN BULLOCK: Hitler, A Study in Tyranny.º *Illus.*
                                                   TB/1123
E. H. CARR: The Twenty Years' Crisis, 1919-1939: *An Introduction to the Study of International Relations*º
                                                   TB/1122
WALTER L. DORN: Competition for Empire, 1740-1763.* *Illus.*   TB/3032
CARL J. FRIEDRICH: The Age of the Baroque, 1610-1660.* *Illus.*   TB/3004
LEO GERSHOY: From Despotism to Revolution, 1763-1789.* *Illus.*   TB/3017
ALBERT GOODWIN: The French Revolution TB/1064
CARLTON J. H. HAYES: A Generation of Materialism, 1871-1900.* *Illus.*   TB/3039
J. H. HEXTER: Reappraisals in History: *New Views on History and Society in Early Modern Europe*
                                                   TB/1100
A. R. HUMPHREYS: The Augustan World: *Society, Thought, and Letters in Eighteenth Century England*
                                                   TB/1105
HANS KOHN, Ed.: The Mind of Modern Russia: *Historical and Political Thought of Russia's Great Age*
                                                   TB/1065
SIR LEWIS NAMIER: Vanished Supremacies: *Essays on European History, 1812-1918*º   TB/1088
JOHN U. NEF: Western Civilization Since the Renaissance: *Peace, War, Industry, and the Arts* TB/1113
FREDERICK L. NUSSBAUM: The Triumph of Science and Reason, 1660-1685.* *Illus.*   TB/3009
RAYMOND W. POSTGATE, Ed.: Revolution from 1789 to 1906: *Selected Documents*   TB/1063
PENFIELD ROBERTS: The Quest for Security, 1715-1740.* *Illus.*   TB/3016
PRISCILLA ROBERTSON: Revolutions of 1848: *A Social History*   TB/1025
ALBERT SOREL: Europe Under the Old Regime. *Translated by Francis H. Herrick*   TB/1121
N. N. SUKHANOV: The Russian Revolution, 1917: *Eyewitness Account. Edited by Joel Carmichael*
                                      Volume I   TB/1066
                                      Volume II TB/1067
JOHN B. WOLF: The Emergence of the Great Powers, 1685-1715.* *Illus.*   TB/3010
JOHN B. WOLF: France: 1814-1919: *The Rise of a Liberal-Democratic Society*   TB/3019

Intellectual History

HERSCHEL BAKER: The Image of Man: *A Study of the Idea of Human Dignity in Classical Antiquity, the Middle Ages, and the Renaissance*   TB/1047
J. BRONOWSKI & BRUCE MAZLISH: The Western Intellectual Tradition: *From Leonardo to Hegel*
                                                   TB/3001

ERNST CASSIRER: The Individual and the Cosmos in Renaissance Philosophy. *Translated with an Introduction by Mario Domandi*   TB/1097
NORMAN COHN: The Pursuit of the Millennium: *Revolutionary Messianism in medieval and Reformation Europe and its bearing on modern Leftist and Rightist totalitarian movements*   TB/1037
ARTHUR O. LOVEJOY: The Great Chain of Being: *A Study of the History of an Idea*   TB/1009
ROBERT PAYNE: Hubris: *A Study of Pride. Foreword by Sir Herbert Read*   TB/1031
BRUNO SNELL: The Discovery of the Mind: *The Greek Origins of European Thought*   TB/1018
ERNEST LEE TUVESON: Millennium and Utopia: *A Study in the Background of the Idea of Progress.* *New Preface by Author*   TB/1134

Literature, Poetry, The Novel & Criticism

JAMES BAIRD: Ishmael: *The Art of Melville in the Contexts of International Primitivism*   TB/1023
JACQUES BARZUN: The House of Intellect TB/1051
W. J. BATE: From Classic to Romantic: *Premises of Taste in Eighteenth Century England*   TB/1036
RACHEL BESPALOFF: On the Iliad   TB/2006
R. P. BLACKMUR, et al.: Lectures in Criticism. *Introduction by Huntington Cairns*   TB/2003
ABRAHAM CAHAN: The Rise of David Levinsky: *a novel. Introduction by John Higham*   TB/1028
ERNST R. CURTIUS: European Literature and the Latin Middle Ages   TB/2015
GEORGE ELIOT: Daniel Deronda: *a novel. Introduction by F. R. Leavis*   TB/1039
ETIENNE GILSON: Dante and Philosophy TB/1089
ALFRED HARBAGE: As They Liked It: *A Study of Shakespeare's Moral Artistry*   TB/1035
STANLEY R. HOPPER, Ed.: Spiritual Problems in Contemporary Literature§   TB/21
A. R. HUMPHREYS: The Augustan World: *Society, Thought, and Letters in Eighteenth Century England*º
                                                   TB/1105
ALDOUS HUXLEY: Antic Hay & The Gioconda Smile.º *Introduction by Martin Green*   TB/3503
ALDOUS HUXLEY: Brave New World & Brave New World Revisited.º *Introduction by C. P. Snow*
                                                   TB/3501
ALDOUS HUXLEY: Point Counter Point.º *Introduction by C. P. Snow*   TB/3502
HENRY JAMES: The Princess Casamassima: *a novel. Introduction by Clinton F. Oliver*   TB/1005
HENRY JAMES: Roderick Hudson: *a novel. Introduction by Leon Edel*   TB/1016
HENRY JAMES: The Tragic Muse: *a novel. Introduction by Leon Edel*   TB/1017
ARNOLD KETTLE: An Introduction to the English Novel. Volume I: *Defoe to George Eliot*   TB/1011
Volume II: *Henry James to the Present*   TB/1012
JOHN STUART MILL: On Bentham and Coleridge. *Introduction by F. R. Leavis*   TB/1070
PERRY MILLER & T. H. JOHNSON, Editors: The Puritans: *A Sourcebook of Their Writings*
                                      Volume I   TB/1093
                                      Volume II TB/1094
KENNETH B. MURDOCK: Literature and Theology in Colonial New England   TB/99
SAMUEL PEPYS: The Diary of Samuel Pepys.º *Edited by O. F. Morshead. Illustrations by Ernest Shepard*
                                                   TB/1007

ST.-JOHN PERSE: Seamarks TB/2002
O. E. RÖLVAAG: Giants in the Earth. *Introduction by Einar Haugen* TB/3504
GEORGE SANTAYANA: Interpretations of Poetry and Religion§ TB/9
C. P. SNOW: Time of Hope: *a novel* TB/1040
DOROTHY VAN GHENT: The English Novel: *Form and Function* TB/1050
E. B. WHITE: One Man's Meat. *Introduction by Walter Blair* TB/3505
MORTON DAUWEN ZABEL, Editor: Literary Opinion in America Volume I TB/3013
Volume II TB/3014

Myth, Symbol & Folklore

JOSEPH CAMPBELL, Editor: Pagan and Christian Mysteries. *Illus.* TB/2013
MIRCEA ELIADE: Cosmos and History: *The Myth of the Eternal Return*§ TB/2050
C. G. JUNG & C. KERÉNYI: Essays on a Science of Mythology: *The Myths of the Divine Child and the Divine Maiden* TB/2014
ERWIN PANOFSKY: Studies in Iconology: *Humanistic Themes in the Art of the Renaissance. 180 illustrations* TB/1077
JEAN SEZNEC: The Survival of the Pagan Gods: *The Mythological Tradition and its Place in Renaissance Humanism and Art. 108 illustrations* TB/2004
HELLMUT WILHELM: Change: *Eight Lectures on the I Ching* TB/2019
HEINRICH ZIMMER: Myths and Symbols in Indian Art and Civilization. *70 illustrations* TB/2005

Philosophy

HENRI BERGSON: Time and Free Will: *An Essay on the Immediate Data of Consciousness*° TB/1021
H. J. BLACKHAM: Six Existentialist Thinkers: *Kierkegaard, Nietzsche, Jaspers, Marcel, Heidegger, Sartre*° TB/1002
ERNST CASSIRER: Rousseau, Kant and Goethe. *Introduction by Peter Gay* TB/1092
FREDERICK COPLESTON: Medieval Philosophy° TB/76
F. M. CORNFORD: From Religion to Philosophy: *A Study in the Origins of Western Speculation*§ TB/20
WILFRID DESAN: The Tragic Finale: *An Essay on the Philosophy of Jean-Paul Sartre* TB/1030
PAUL FRIEDLÄNDER: Plato: *An Introduction* TB/2017
ETIENNE GILSON: Dante and Philosophy TB/1089
WILLIAM CHASE GREENE: Moira: *Fate, Good, and Evil in Greek Thought* TB/1104
W. K. C. GUTHRIE: The Greek Philosophers: *From Thales to Aristotle*° TB/1008
F. H. HEINEMANN: Existentialism and the Modern Predicament TB/28
IMMANUEL KANT: The Doctrine of Virtue, *being Part II of The Metaphysic of Morals. Translated with Notes and Introduction by Mary J. Gregor. Foreword by H. J. Paton* TB/110
IMMANUEL KANT: Lectures on Ethics.§ *Introduction by Lewis W. Beck* TB/105
WILLARD VAN ORMAN QUINE: From a Logical Point of View: *Logico-Philosophical Essays* TB/566

BERTRAND RUSSELL et al.: The Philosophy of Bertrand Russell. *Edited by Paul Arthur Schilpp*
Volume I TB/1095
Volume II TB/1096
L. S. STEBBING: A Modern Introduction to Logic TB/538
ALFRED NORTH WHITEHEAD: Process and Reality: *An Essay in Cosmology* TB/1033
WILHELM WINDELBAND: A History of Philosophy I: *Greek, Roman, Medieval* TB/38
WILHELM WINDELBAND: A History of Philosophy II: *Renaissance, Enlightenment, Modern* TB/39

Philosophy of History

NICOLAS BERDYAEV: The Beginning and the End§ TB/14
NICOLAS BERDYAEV: The Destiny of Man TB/61
WILHELM DILTHEY: Pattern and Meaning in History: *Thoughts on History and Society.*° *Edited with an Introduction by H. P. Rickman* TB/1075
RAYMOND KLIBANSKY & H. J. PATON, Eds.: Philosophy and History: *The Ernst Cassirer Festschrift. Illus.* TB/1115
JOSE ORTEGA Y GASSET: The Modern Theme. *Introduction by Jose Ferrater Mora* TB/1038
KARL R. POPPER: The Poverty of Historicism° TB/1126
W. H. WALSH: Philosophy of History: *An Introduction* TB/1020

Political Science & Government

JEREMY BENTHAM: The Handbook of Political Fallacies: *Introduction by Crane Brinton* TB/1069
KENNETH E. BOULDING: Conflict and Defense: *A General Theory* TB/3024
CRANE BRINTON: English Political Thought in the Nineteenth Century TB/1071
EDWARD S. CORWIN: American Constitutional History: *Essays edited by Alpheus T. Mason and Gerald Garvey* TB/1136
ROBERT DAHL & CHARLES E. LINDBLOM: Politics, Economics, and Welfare: *Planning and Politico-Economic Systems Resolved into Basic Social Processes* TB/3037
JOHN NEVILLE FIGGIS: Political Thought from Gerson to Grotius: 1414-1625: *Seven Studies. Introduction by Garrett Mattingly* TB/1032
F. L. GANSHOF: Feudalism TB/1058
G. P. GOOCH: English Democratic Ideas in the Seventeenth Century TB/1006
ROBERT H. JACKSON: The Supreme Court in the American System of Government TB/1106
DAN N. JACOBS, Ed.: The New Communist Manifesto *and Related Documents* TB/1078
DAN N. JACOBS & HANS BAERWALD, Eds.: Chinese Communism: *Selected Documents* TB/3031
ROBERT GREEN McCLOSKEY: American Conservatism in the Age of Enterprise, 1865-1910 TB/1137
KINGSLEY MARTIN: French Liberal Thought in the Eighteenth Century: *A Study of Political Ideas from Bayle to Condorcet* TB/1114
JOHN STUART MILL: On Bentham and Coleridge. *Introduction by F. R. Leavis* TB/1070
JOHN B. MORRALL: Political Thought in Medieval Times TB/1076

5

KARL R. POPPER: The Open Society and Its Enemies
Volume I: *The Spell of Plato* TB/1101
Volume II: *The High Tide of Prophecy: Hegel, Marx, and the Aftermath* TB/1102
JOSEPH A. SCHUMPETER: Capitalism, Socialism and Democracy TB/3008

Psychology

ALFRED ADLER: Problems of Neurosis. *Introduction by Heinz L. Ansbacher* TB/1145
ANTON T. BOISEN: The Exploration of the Inner World: *A Study of Mental Disorder and Religious Experience* TB/87
LEON FESTINGER, HENRY W. RIECKEN, STANLEY SCHACHTER: When Prophecy Fails: *A Social and Psychological Study of a Modern Group that Predicted the Destruction of the World* ▌ TB/1132
SIGMUND FREUD: On Creativity and the Unconscious: *Papers on the Psychology of Art, Literature, Love, Religion.§ Intro. by Benjamin Nelson* TB/45
C. JUDSON HERRICK: The Evolution of Human Nature TB/545
ALDOUS HUXLEY: The Devils of Loudun: *A Study in the Psychology of Power Politics and Mystical Religion in the France of Cardinal Richelieu*§° TB/60
WILLIAM JAMES: Psychology: *The Briefer Course. Edited with an Intro. by Gordon Allport* TB/1034
C. G. JUNG: Psychological Reflections. *Edited by Jolande Jacobi* TB/2001
C. G. JUNG: Symbols of Transformation: *An Analysis of the Prelude to a Case of Schizophrenia. Illus.*
Volume I TB/2009
Volume II TB/2010
C. G. JUNG & C. KERÉNYI: Essays on a Science of Mythology: *The Myths of the Divine Child and the Divine Maiden* TB/2014
SOREN KIERKEGAARD: Repetition: *An Essay in Experimental Psychology. Translated with Introduction & Notes by Walter Lowrie* TB/117
KARL MENNINGER: Theory of Psychoanalytic Technique TB/1144
ERICH NEUMANN: Amor and Psyche: *The Psychic Development of the Feminine* TB/2012
ERICH NEUMANN: The Origins and History of Consciousness Volume I *Illus.* TB/2007
Volume II TB/2008
C. P. OBERNDORF: A History of Psychoanalysis in America TB/1147
JEAN PIAGET, BÄRBEL INHELDER, & ALINA SZEMINSKA: The Child's Conception of Geometry TB/1146

RELIGION

Ancient & Classical

J. H. BREASTED: Development of Religion and Thought in Ancient Egypt. *Introduction by John A. Wilson* TB/57
HENRI FRANKFORT: Ancient Egyptian Religion: *An Interpretation* TB/77
WILLIAM CHASE GREENE: Moira: *Fate, Good and Evil in Greek Thought* TB/1104

G. RACHEL LEVY: Religious Conceptions of the Stone Age *and their Influence upon European Thought. Illus. Introduction by Henri Frankfort* TB/106
MARTIN P. NILSSON: Greek Folk Religion. *Foreword by Arthur Darby Nock* TB/78
ALEXANDRE PIANKOFF: The Shrines of Tut-Ankh-Amon. *Edited by N. Rambova. 117 illus.* TB/2011
H. J. ROSE: Religion in Greece and Rome TB/55

Biblical Thought & Literature

W. F. ALBRIGHT: The Biblical Period from Abraham to Ezra TB/102
C. K. BARRETT, Ed.: The New Testament Background: *Selected Documents* TB/86
C. H. DODD: The Authority of the Bible TB/43
M. S. ENSLIN: Christian Beginnings TB/5
M. S. ENSLIN: The Literature of the Christian Movement TB/6
H. E. FOSDICK: A Guide to Understanding the Bible TB/2
H. H. ROWLEY: The Growth of the Old Testament TB/107
D. WINTON THOMAS, Ed.: Documents from Old Testament Times TB/85

Christianity: Origins & Early Development

ADOLF DEISSMANN: Paul: *A Study in Social and Religious History* TB/15
EDWARD GIBBON: The Triumph of Christendom in the Roman Empire (*Chaps. XV-XX of "Decline and Fall," J. B. Bury edition*).§ *Illus.* TB/46
MAURICE GOGUEL: Jesus and the Origins of Christianity.° *Introduction by C. Leslie Mitton*
Volume I: *Prolegomena to the Life of Jesus* TB/65
Volume II: *The Life of Jesus* TB/66
EDGAR J. GOODSPEED: A Life of Jesus TB/1
ADOLF HARNACK: The Mission and Expansion of Christianity *in the First Three Centuries. Introduction by Jaroslav Pelikan* TB/92
R. K. HARRISON: The Dead Sea Scrolls: *An Introduction*° TB/84
EDWIN HATCH: The Influence of Greek Ideas on Christianity.§ *Introduction and Bibliography by Frederick C. Grant* TB /18
ARTHUR DARBY NOCK: Early Gentile Christianity and Its Hellenistic Background TB/111
ARTHUR DARBY NOCK: St. Paul° TB/104
JOHANNES WEISS: Earliest Christianity: *A History of the Period A.D. 30-150. Introduction and Bibliography by Frederick C. Grant* Volume I TB/53
Volume II TB/54

Christianity: The Middle Ages, The Reformation, and After

G. P. FEDOTOV: The Russian Religious Mind: *Kievan Christianity, the tenth to the thirteenth centuries* TB/70
ÉTIENNE GILSON: Dante and Philosophy TB/1089
WILLIAM HALLER: The Rise of Puritanism TB/22
JOHAN HUIZINGA: Erasmus and the Age of Reformation. *Illus.* TB/19

JOHN T. McNEILL: Makers of Christianity: *From Alfred the Great to Schleiermacher*   TB/121

A. C. McGIFFERT: Protestant Thought Before Kant. *Preface by Jaroslav Pelikan*   TB/93

KENNETH B. MURDOCK: Literature and Theology in Colonial New England   TB/99

GORDON RUPP: Luther's Progress to the Diet of Worms°   TB/120

Judaic Thought & Literature

MARTIN BUBER: Eclipse of God: *Studies in the Relation Between Religion and Philosophy*   TB/12

MARTIN BUBER: Moses: *The Revelation and the Covenant*   TB/27

MARTIN BUBER: Pointing the Way. *Introduction by Maurice S. Friedman*   TB/103

MARTIN BUBER: The Prophetic Faith   TB/73

MARTIN BUBER: Two Types of Faith: *the interpenetration of Judaism and Christianity*°   TB/75

MAURICE S. FRIEDMAN: Martin Buber: *The Life of Dialogue*   TB/64

FLAVIUS JOSEPHUS: The Great Roman-Jewish War, *with The Life of Josephus. Introduction by William R. Farmer*   TB/74

T. J. MEEK: Hebrew Origins   TB/69

Oriental Religions: Far Eastern, Near Eastern

TOR ANDRAE: Mohammed: *The Man and His Faith*   TB/62

EDWARD CONZE: Buddhism: *Its Essence and Development.*° *Foreword by Arthur Waley*   TB/58

EDWARD CONZE, et al., Editors: Buddhist Texts Through the Ages   TB/113

ANANDA COOMARASWAMY: Buddha and the Gospel of Buddhism   TB/119

H. G. CREEL: Confucius and the Chinese Way   TB/63

FRANKLIN EDGERTON, Trans. & Ed.: The Bhagavad Gita   TB/115

SWAMI NIKHILANANDA, Trans. & Ed.: The Upanishads: *A One-Volume Abridgment*   TB/114

HELLMUT WILHELM: Change: *Eight Lectures on the I Ching*   TB/2019

Philosophy of Religion

RUDOLF BULTMANN: History and Eschatology: *The Presence of Eternity*   TB/91

RUDOLF BULTMANN AND FIVE CRITICS: Kerygma and Myth: *A Theological Debate*   TB/80

RUDOLF BULTMANN and KARL KUNDSIN: Form Criticism: *Two Essays on New Testament Research. Translated by Frederick C. Grant*   TB/96

MIRCEA ELIADE: The Sacred and the Profane   TB/81

LUDWIG FEUERBACH: The Essence of Christianity.§ *Introduction by Karl Barth. Foreword by H. Richard Niebuhr*   TB/11

ADOLF HARNACK: What is Christianity?§ *Introduction by Rudolf Bultmann*   TB/17

FRIEDRICH HEGEL: On Christianity: *Early Theological Writings. Edited by Richard Kroner and T. M. Knox*   TB/79

KARL HEIM: Christian Faith and Natural Science TB/16

IMMANUEL KANT: Religion Within the Limits of Reason Alone.§ *Introduction by Theodore M. Greene and John Silber*   TB/67

PIERRE TEILHARD DE CHARDIN: The Phenomenon of Man°   TB/83

Religion, Culture & Society

JOSEPH L. BLAU, Ed.: Cornerstones of Religious Freedom in America: *Selected Basic Documents, Court Decisions and Public Statements. Enlarged and revised edition, with new Introduction by the Editor*   TB/118

C. C. GILLISPIE: Genesis and Geology: *The Decades before Darwin*§   TB/51

BENJAMIN NELSON: Religious Traditions and the Spirit of Capitalism: *From the Church Fathers to Jeremy Bentham*   TB/1130

H. RICHARD NIEBUHR: Christ and Culture   TB/3

H. RICHARD NIEBUHR: The Kingdom of God in America   TB/49

RALPH BARTON PERRY: Puritanism and Democracy   TB/1138

WALTER RAUSCHENBUSCH: Christianity and the Social Crisis.‡ *Edited by Robert D. Cross*   TB/3059

KURT SAMUELSSON: Religion and Economic Action: *A Critique of Max Weber's The Protestant Ethic and the Spirit of Capitalism.*⫶° *Trans. by E. G. French; Ed. with Intro. by D. C. Coleman*   TB/1131

ERNST TROELTSCH: The Social Teaching of the Christian Churches.° *Introduction by H. Richard Niebuhr*   Volume I TB/71
    Volume II TB/72

Religious Thinkers & Traditions

AUGUSTINE: An Augustine Synthesis. *Edited by Erich Przywara*   TB/35

KARL BARTH: Church Dogmatics: *A Selection. Introduction by H. Gollwitzer; Edited by G. W. Bromiley*   TB/95

KARL BARTH: Dogmatics in Outline   TB/56

KARL BARTH: The Word of God and the Word of Man   TB/13

THOMAS CORBISHLEY, s. j.: Roman Catholicism   TB/112

ADOLF DEISSMANN: Paul: *A Study in Social and Religious History*   TB/15

JOHANNES ECKHART: Meister Eckhart: *A Modern Translation by R. B. Blakney*   TB/8

WINTHROP HUDSON: The Great Tradition of the American Churches   TB/98

SOREN KIERKEGAARD: Edifying Discourses. *Edited with an Introduction by Paul Holmer*   TB/32

SOREN KIERKEGAARD: The Journals of Kierkegaard.° *Edited with an Introduction by Alexander Dru*   TB/52

SOREN KIERKEGAARD: The Point of View for My Work as an Author: *A Report to History.*§ *Preface by Benjamin Nelson*   TB/88

SOREN KIERKEGAARD: The Present Age.§ *Translated and edited by Alexander Dru. Introduction by Walter Kaufmann*   TB/94

SOREN KIERKEGAARD: Purity of Heart. *Translated by Douglas Steere*   TB/4

SOREN KIERKEGAARD: Repetition: *An Essay in Experimental Psychology. Translated with Introduction & Notes by Walter Lowrie*   TB/117

SOREN KIERKEGAARD: Works of Love: *Some Christian Reflections in the Form of Discourses*   TB/122

7

WALTER LOWRIE: Kierkegaard: *A Life*
Volume I   TB/89
Volume II   TB/90
GABRIEL MARCEL: Homo Viator: *Introduction to a Metaphysic of Hope*   TB/97
PERRY MILLER: Errand into the Wilderness   TB/1139
PERRY MILLER & T. H. JOHNSON, Editors: The Puritans: *A Sourcebook of Their Writings*
Volume I   TB/1093
Volume II   TB/1094
PAUL PFUETZE: Self, Society, Existence: *Human Nature and Dialogue in the Thought of George Herbert Mead and Martin Buber*   TB/1059
F. SCHLEIERMACHER: The Christian Faith. *Introduction by Richard R. Niebuhr*   Volume I   TB/108
Volume II   TB/109
F. SCHLEIERMACHER: On Religion: *Speeches to Its Cultured Despisers. Intro. by Rudolf Otto*   TB/36
PAUL TILLICH: Dynamics of Faith   TB/42
EVELYN UNDERHILL: Worship   TB/10
G. VAN DER LEEUW: Religion in Essence and Manifestation: *A Study in Phenomenology. Appendices by Hans H. Penner*   Volume I   TB/100
Volume II   TB/101

NATURAL SCIENCES
AND MATHEMATICS

Biological Sciences

CHARLOTTE AUERBACH: The Science of Genetics∑
TB/568
A. BELLAIRS: Reptiles: *Life History, Evolution, and Structure. Illus.*   TB/520
LUDWIG VON BERTALANFFY: Modern Theories of Development: *An Introduction to Theoretical Biology*   TB/554
LUDWIG VON BERTALANFFY: Problems of Life: *An Evaluation of Modern Biological and Scientific Thought*   TB/521
JOHN TYLER BONNER: The Ideas of Biology.∑ *Illus.*
TB/570
HAROLD F. BLUM: Time's Arrow and Evolution
TB/555
A. J. CAIN: Animal Species and their Evolution. *Illus.*
TB/519
WALTER B. CANNON: Bodily Changes in Pain, Hunger, Fear and Rage. *Illus.*   TB/562
W. E. LE GROS CLARK: The Antecedents of Man: *An Introduction to the Evolution of the Primates.° Illus.*
TB/559
W. H. DOWDESWELL: Animal Ecology. *Illus.* TB/543
W. H. DOWDESWELL: The Mechanism of Evolution. *Illus.*   TB/527
R. W. GERARD: Unresting Cells. *Illus.*   TB/541
DAVID LACK: Darwin's Finches. *Illus.*   TB/544
J. E. MORTON: Molluscs: *An Introduction to their Form and Functions. Illus.*   TB/529
ADOLF PORTMANN: Animals as Social Beings.° *Illus.*
TB/572
O. W. RICHARDS: The Social Insects. *Illus.*   TB/542
P. M. SHEPPARD: Natural Selection and Heredity. *Illus.*   TB/528
EDMUND W. SINNOTT: Cell and Psyche: *The Biology of Purpose*   TB/546
C. H. WADDINGTON: How Animals Develop. *Illus.*
TB/553

Chemistry

J. R. PARTINGTON: A Short History of Chemistry. *Illus.*   TB/522
J. READ: A Direct Entry to Organic Chemistry. *Illus.*
TB/523
J. READ: Through Alchemy to Chemistry. *Illus.* TB/561

Geography

R. E. COKER: This Great and Wide Sea: *An Introduction to Oceanography and Marine Biology. Illus.*
TB/551
F. K. HARE: The Restless Atmosphere   TB/560

History of Science

W. DAMPIER, Ed.: Readings in the Literature of Science. *Illus.*   TB/512
A. HUNTER DUPREE: Science in the Federal Government: *A History of Policies and Activities to 1940*
TB/573
ALEXANDRE KOYRÉ: From the Closed World to the Infinite Universe: *Copernicus, Kepler, Galileo, Newton, etc.*   TB/31
A. G. VAN MELSEN: From Atomos to Atom: *A History of the Concept Atom*   TB/517
O. NEUGEBAUER: The Exact Sciences in Antiquity
TB/552
H. T. PLEDGE: Science Since 1500: *A Short History of Mathematics, Physics, Chemistry and Biology. Illus.*
TB/506
GEORGE SARTON: Ancient Science and Modern Civilization   TB/501
HANS THIRRING: Energy for Man: *From Windmills to Nuclear Power*   TB/556
WILLIAM LAW WHYTE: Essay on Atomism: *From Democritus to 1960*   TB/565
A. WOLF: A History of Science, Technology and Philosophy in the 16th and 17th Centuries.° *Illus.*
Volume I   TB/508
Volume II   TB/509
A. WOLF: A History of Science, Technology, and Philosophy in the Eighteenth Century.° *Illus.*
Volume I   TB/539
Volume II   TB/540

Mathematics

H. DAVENPORT: The Higher Arithmetic: *An Introduction to the Theory of Numbers*   TB/526
H. G. FORDER: Geometry: *An Introduction*   TB/548
GOTTLOB FREGE: The Foundations of Arithmetic: *A Logico-Mathematical Enquiry into the Concept of Number*   TB/534
S. KÖRNER: The Philosophy of Mathematics: *An Introduction*   TB/547
D. E. LITTLEWOOD: Skeleton Key of Mathematics: *A Simple Account of Complex Algebraic Problems*
TB/525
GEORGE E. OWEN: Fundamentals of Scientific Mathematics   TB/569
WILLARD VAN ORMAN QUINE: Mathematical Logic
TB/558
O. G. SUTTON: Mathematics in Action.° *Foreword by James R. Newman. Illus.*   TB/518
FREDERICK WAISMANN: Introduction to Mathematical Thinking. *Foreword by Karl Menger*   TB/511

Philosophy of Science

R. B. BRAITHWAITE: Scientific Explanation   TB/515

J. BRONOWSKI: Science and Human Values. *Illus.*
    TB/505

ALBERT EINSTEIN: Philosopher-Scientist. *Edited by Paul A. Schilpp*   Volume I TB/502
    Volume II TB/503

WERNER HEISENBERG: Physics and Philosophy: *The Revolution in Modern Science. Introduction by F. S. C. Northrop*   TB/549

JOHN MAYNARD KEYNES: A Treatise on Probability.° *Introduction by N. R. Hanson*   TB/557

STEPHEN TOULMIN: Foresight and Understanding: *An Enquiry into the Aims of Science. Foreword by Jacques Barzun*   TB/564

STEPHEN TOULMIN: The Philosophy of Science: *An Introduction*   TB/513

G. J. WHITROW: The Natural Philosophy of Time°
    TB/563

Physics and Cosmology

DAVID BOHM: Causality and Chance in Modern Physics. *Foreword by Louis de Broglie*   TB/536

P. W. BRIDGMAN: The Nature of Thermodynamics
    TB/537

A. C. CROMBIE, Ed.: Turning Point in Physics TB/535

C. V. DURELL: Readable Relativity. *Foreword by Freeman J. Dyson*   TB/530

ARTHUR EDDINGTON: Space, Time and Gravitation: *An outline of the General Relativity Theory* TB/510

GEORGE GAMOW: Biography of PhysicsΣ   TB/567

MAX JAMMER: Concepts of Force: *A Study in the Foundation of Dynamics*   TB/550

MAX JAMMER: Concepts of Mass *in Classical and Modern Physics*   TB/571

MAX JAMMER: Concepts of Space: *The History of Theories of Space in Physics. Foreword by Albert Einstein*   TB/533

EDMUND WHITTAKER: History of the Theories of Aether and Electricity
    Volume I: *The Classical Theories* TB/531
    Volume II: *The Modern Theories* TB/532

G. J. WHITROW: The Structure and Evolution of the Universe: *An Introduction to Cosmology. Illus.*
    TB/504

9

A LETTER TO THE READER

Overseas, there is considerable belief that we are a country of extreme conservatism and that we cannot accommodate to social change.

Books about America in the hands of readers abroad can help change those ideas.

The U. S. Information Agency cannot, by itself, meet the vast need for books about the United States.

You can help.

Harper Torchbooks provides three packets of books on American history, economics, sociology, literature and politics to help meet the need.

To send a packet of Torchbooks [*] overseas, all you need do is send your check for $7 (which includes cost of shipping) to Harper & Row. The U. S. Information Agency will distribute the books to libraries, schools, and other centers all over the world.

I ask every American to support this program, part of a worldwide BOOKS USA campaign.

I ask you to share in the opportunity to help tell others about America.

EDWARD R. MURROW
Director,
U. S. Information Agency

[*retailing at $10.85 to $12.00]

PACKET I: *Twentieth Century America*

Dulles/America's Rise to World Power, 1898-1954
Cochran/The American Business System, 1900-1955
Zabel, Editor/Literary Opinion in America (two volumes)
Drucker/The New Society: *The Anatomy of Industrial Order*
Fortune Editors/America in the Sixties: *The Economy and the Society*

PACKET II: *American History*

Billington/The Far Western Frontier, 1830-1860
Mowry/The Era of Theodore Roosevelt and the
    Birth of Modern America, 1900-1912
Faulkner/Politics, Reform, and Expansion, 1890-1900
Cochran & Miller/The Age of Enterprise: *A Social History of
    Industrial America*
Tyler/Freedom's Ferment: *American Social History from the
    Revolution to the Civil War*

PACKET III: *American History*

Hansen/The Atlantic Migration, 1607-1860
Degler/Out of Our Past: *The Forces that Shaped Modern America*
Probst, Editor/The Happy Republic: *A Reader in Tocqueville's America*
Alden/The American Revolution, 1775-1783
Wright/The Cultural Life of the American Colonies, 1607-1763

*Your gift will be acknowledged directly to you by the overseas recipient.
Simply fill out the coupon, detach and mail with your check or money order.*

NOTE: *This offer expires December 31, 1966.*